The House of Habsburg

THE HOUSE OF HABSBURG

Six Hundred Years of a European Dynasty

ADAM WANDRUSZKA

*Translated from the original German
by Cathleen and Hans Epstein*

GREENWOOD PRESS, PUBLISHERS
WESTPORT, CONNECTICUT

Library of Congress Cataloging in Publication Data

Wandruszka, Adam, 1914-
    The House of Habsburg.

    Translation of Das Haus Habsburg.
    Reprint of the ed. published by Doubleday, Garden
City, N. Y.
    Bibliography: p.
    Includes index.
    1. Habsburg, House of.   I.   Title.
[DB36.1.W313 1975]   929.7'3   75-5004
ISBN 0-8371-7928-9

The *House of Habsburg* was originally published
in German by Friedrich Vorwerk Verlag Stuttgart
under the title *Das Haus Habsburg:*
Die Geschichte einer europäischen Dynastie.

Copyright © 1964 by Doubleday & Company, Inc.

This edition originally published in 1964 by Doubleday &
Company, Inc., Garden City, N.Y.

Reprinted with the permission of Doubleday & Company, Inc.

Reprinted in 1975 by Greenwood Press, Inc.
51 Riverside Avenue, Westport, CT 06880

Library of Congress catalog card number 75-5004
ISBN 0-8371-7928-9

Printed in the United States of America

10 9 8 7 6 5 4 3 2

Preface

The present book was undertaken at the suggestion of its original publisher, Mr. Friedrich Vorwerk of Stuttgart. Though I accepted the task gladly, I realized from the beginning the difficulties and dangers inherent in treating such an exhaustive subject in a relatively modest compass, instead of in several volumes, which might even then have remained incomplete. But there is a challenge in steering the right course between the shallows of superficiality and improper generalization, and the rocks of excessive detail.

I wish to return my sincerest thanks to Professor Alphons Lhotsky, of the University of Vienna, for his frequent friendly advice, criticism, and suggestions, offered while he watched over my progress. Further, I must gratefully acknowledge the various suggestions and references provided by Professors Heinrich Benedikt, Hugo Hantsch, Heinrich von Fichtenau, and Erich Zöllner, all of the University of Vienna; Dr. Anna Coreth (Countess Coreth), Dr. Erika Weinzierl-Fischer, and Dr. Rudolf Neck, all of the Vienna State Archive; my friend and former fellow student, Professor Dietrich W. H. Schwarz, of the University of Zürich; and my brother, Dr. Mario Wandruszka, Professor at the University of Tübingen. The specialist will recognize how much my general outlook owes to my late, unforgettable teacher, Heinrich Ritter von Srbik, and to the pioneering research of Otto Brunner (at present at the University of Hamburg).

Adam Wandruszka
Vienna, Summer 1956

Preface to the Second Edition

The preparation of a second edition has become necessary sooner than was expected. The interest of the general public was matched by the almost entirely positive reception of the book by scholarly critics and journalists alike. While this was not unexpected in Austria and southern and southwestern Germany, where such a book was genuinely needed, I was surprised that such particularly lively approbation was voiced in Switzerland, the Netherlands, and northern Germany, areas whose view of history has been considerably influenced by their struggle against the House of Habsburg. The appreciative judgment most pleasing to me was that of the Benedictines exiled from Braunau in Czechoslovakia, and now settled in Rohr, Bavaria, who chose the book to be read aloud to them at meals.

The new edition has given me an opportunity to correct some slips, which were almost unavoidable in the treatment of such an extensive subject, and to amplify some points in the text and in the bibliography as a result of recent publications.

I owe most sincere thanks to all competent critics and reviewers who have enabled me to make these corrections and to supply supplementary details. My thanks are also due to Mr. Adolf Peter Koof, a student who helped me with the proofreading of the second edition.

Adam Wandruszka
Cologne, Summer 1959

Contents

List of Maps

Introduction

"Austria," Hermann Bahr once wrote, "has not been lucky with its biographers." Bahr, one of the most sensitive men of letters of twentieth-century Austria, pondered over the image of the Austrian monarchy in history and lamented the fact that it was predominantly negative. He was right. Historians in an age of nationalism and liberalism had not much good to write about that old dynastic structure which, as Francis Joseph himself knew, was an "anomaly." Austria's history was written, mostly by "renegade Austrians" looking toward Prussia-Germany, as an "act of revenge." And then there were the so-called "Whig historians" who had little understanding for the "ramshackle Empire," who saw in it no more than the "prison of peoples." Thus a strange alliance —by no means a holy one—between the pro-German nationalists and Western liberals sat in judgment over a centuries-old monarchy. It helped set the stage for the final debunking act, when the very name of Austria was abolished by the decree of the fiercest of all "renegade Austrians," to whom Habsburg history had been blatant "treason" against the German people. In 1938 he had his "act of revenge."

There is no call for nostalgia over the Empire that vanished in 1918. Ramshackle it certainly was, and the shadows of decline had long settled over it. And Francis Joseph, fatherly, fumbling, but stubborn, still held the Empire together by his mere will alone. It was his death that finally released his peoples. They had to break away sooner or later. Today, however, various historical questions remain: what was the vanished Empire like, what were its origins, what was its "mission" and achievement? These questions take us back into an age of medieval and early modern dynasticism, back to the Holy Roman Empire whose crown the Habsburgs carried almost uninterruptedly for nearly five centuries and whose defense they provided against West and East; they take us into the Central European area in which down to our own day the peoples, religions, and cultures are richly intermixed.

A political question also remains, a vital one. The imperial Austrian tradition was a supranational one, not a merely German one. And the rulers of Austria and their advisers had to deal with the problems of a multinational area which in its origins had been a voluntary association of different historical units. The old . . . *tu felix Austria nube* may no longer have meant much to the ethnically self-conscious nationalities of the nineteenth-century monarchy. But certainly the associational, voluntaristic element in Habsburg empire building, established by the marriage policy and repeatedly reinforced by the vote of the different Estates, remained a fundamental tradition in nineteenth-century Austria. In spite of a record of occasional senseless centralization and oppression (even though Francis Joseph's *viribus unitis* often amounted in effect to a *divide et impera* policy over his various nationalities) the Habsburg Empire was ultimately immune against becoming a "prison of peoples." Its rationale throughout had been not conquest but power, its guiding idea not the imposition of one national culture on others but a renunciation of nationalist aspiration which Franz Werfel has called the *sacrificium nationis*. And its undoing in the last analysis was not hubris—though an element of hubris there may have been during the last decade before the First World War in the monarchy's policy toward Serbia—but a longstanding unwillingness as well as inability to become fully a modern state.

Since the catastrophe in 1918 the problem of Austria has been variously reviewed. While statesmen like Sir Winston

Churchill with a sense of remorse lamented the "complete breakup" of an Empire that, after all, had afforded a "common life, with advantages of trade and security," political scientists like Joseph Redlich paved the way for an analysis of the unique and intricate political and administrative structure of the monarchy. The Viennese school of historians spearheaded by Oswald Redlich has come forth with a whole library of excellent studies on the Austrian past. Even in the so-called *"gesamtdeutsche,"* fundamentally Germano-centered histories of Austria of the nineteen thirties, and even in present-day studies of imperial Austria emanating from the succession states now behind the Iron Curtain, the ninteenth-century emphasis on Austria as the villain has given way to a genuine attempt at understanding its historical role.

Adam Wandruszka, professor of modern history at the University of Cologne, is a product of the Viennese school of historians and a student of Heinrich von Srbik. He has made a name for himself with a penetrating study of the political structure of the first Austrian Republic which forms part of the standard work in the field.[1] The dynastic—or, we might say, "biographical"—approach to Austrian history in this volume is particularly appropriate for an imaginative re-creation of the Austrian past. If the usual statist and national approach is unsatisfactory for a treatment of European history at large, it is particularly unsuitable for imperial Austria. The political reality in the monarchy was the Habsburg dynasty. The land "Austria" was, strictly speaking, the duchy that the sons of Rudolf I obtained as fief in 1282. This Austria was the core of the Habsburg *Hausmacht*; in an ever-growing, rambling Empire it remained the land, the base of the family. At the same time "Austria" kept expanding as the dynasty acquired new territory. "Austria" in history therefore had little identity. It was not a nation, never quite a state; it

[1] *Geschichte der Republik Oesterreich*, ed. by Heinrich Benedikt. Munich, 1954.

was part of a kaleidoscopic world, within which crowns German, Burgundian, Spanish, Danubian, Italian played their parts. It was ever-changing, ever re-emerging with a different shape and coloring. And its continuity was the dynasty, transcending time and space, transcending itself ultimately after 1740 when Charles VI, the last Habsburg in the male succession, died. The various meanings of the famous motto of Frederick III, A.E.I.O.U. (*Austriae est imperare orbi universo* and later *Austria erit in orbe ultima*), have thus in a strange way found fulfillment in the history of the House of Habsburg down to the year 1918.

The history of the House of Habsburg from Rudolf I's election in 1273 as German king to the early eighteenth century is above all a record of creativity, flexibility and a carefully developed gift for utilizing situations. The "historical instinct," the "ability to cope," which Hugo von Hofmannsthal detected in the Austrians of his own day, were qualities that Habsburg history had developed. Whereas the Hohenstaufen dynasty ultimately succumbed to the consequences of its own rigid anti-papal policy, the "pious" Count Rudolf, whose election as German king put an end to the disastrous interregnum in the Holy Roman Empire, embarked upon a new course designed to strengthen the Empire and his House through co-operation with the Church. Thus he set the tune for the Habsburg policies toward Rome for more than six centuries. Rudolf furthermore, by arranging the double wedding between his children and those of his foe, the Premyslid Ottokar II, established a pattern for a Danubian dynastic alignment that was finally realized some two hundred and fifty years later through the marriage arrangements between Maximilian I and the Jagellon king Vladislav II of Bohemia and Hungary. The year 1526, when Vladislav's son Louis II died in battle (Mohács) against the Turks and when the Estates elected Archduke Ferdinand King of Bohemia and Hungary, was decisive for the consolidation in the Danubian area of the

House of Austria. Thus began its "heroic" age. It became, in the words of Joseph Redlich, a "European power," just as, through the Burgundian and Spanish inheritances of Emperor Charles V, Ferdinand's brother, it became a "world power." It has been rightly pointed out that in Central Europe marriages between reigning houses had been so common for more than a century that at least two Danubian states at a given time were combined in a personal union.

Even though the dynasty was seriously challenged with the failure of Charles V, with the Peace of Westphalia, and eventually with the extinction of the Spanish Habsburg line, its creativeness was by no means "exhausted," as A. J. P. Taylor claims. Setbacks for the Habsburg position as a "world power," setbacks for the Holy Roman Empire were remedied by consolidation in southeastern Europe: re-Catholization, the defense of the west against the Turks who were in alliance with the French kingdom, and finally reconquest of Hungary from the Turks.

By 1687 all the monarchy's component crowns, the crowns of St. Leopold (for the Austrian hereditary lands), St. Wenceslas (for Bohemia), St. Stephen (for Hungary) were hereditary. And Charles VI's Pragmatic Sanction, finally approved by all the Estates, assured that his lands were henceforth to be joined *indivisibiliter et inseparabiliter*. It made out of a personal union among the Habsburg lands a real union and thus became "the firm, legal basis of the first continental power of Europe" (Joseph Redlich). In the late seventeenth and early eighteenth centuries the *Monarchia Austriaca*, by no means an anachronism, emerged in its Central European concentration as a reinforced power. Indeed, in its struggle against the Turks, it was Europe.

The "problematic age" (Joseph Redlich) of the Habsburg monarchy reaches back into the late eighteenth century. The fear of the Turks, which had been a vital cohesive element in the Empire, receded. And in the late eighteenth century, the age of Maria Theresa and in particular of Joseph II, a dilemma appeared which remained basic to nineteenth-century Austria. The rambling, haphazard administration of the Empire became increasingly cumbersome, and the survival of the monarchy depended on its ability to develop a unitary bureaucracy that would strengthen the "state." At the same time, centralization, the "state," was bound to offend the historical traditions of the different Habsburg possessions. Bureaucratic absolutism and the supranational tradition, rational Josephinist Austria and historically grown Austria, turned out to be conflicting elements. The main ideas that grew out of the French Revolution, nationalism and democracy, called into question the very *raison d'être* of the Habsburg monarchy. Under these conditions the traditional Habsburg creativity gave way to drift. Nevertheless, the Empire in its last century kept displaying a striking degree of resilience. It has been called the "toughest organization in the history of modern Europe" (*The Times Literary Supplement*, April 27, 1951). It was tough, almost callous, in its ability to take defeats, to experiment with constitutions (until the Austro-Hungarian Compromise in 1867), prime ministers, policies. And its "condition of incurable disunion," as a shrewd observer (Mark Twain) remarked, kept maintaining at least a negative balance of sorts and remained to the end a source of strength for the government.

Francisco-Josephinian Vienna, was, according to Karl Kraus an "experimental station for world declines" (*Experimentieranstalt für Weltuntergänge*). If Kraus was correct, the dying Empire reflected, indeed anticipated, the problems, cultural and political, pertaining to twentieth-century man. Behind the façade of an amusing, carefree life and of playful elegance there appeared early signs of uneasiness and self-doubt. Imperial Austria at the turn of the century sensed acutely, as Hugo von Hofmannsthal put it, that "the whole was threatened," that the center could not hold. It is not accidental therefore that in this atmosphere of a pioneering skepticism concerning conventional reality, a new reality—the subconscious—should have been discovered (Schnitzler, Freud); a new novel (Kafka, Musil), philosophy (Wittgenstein), music (Schönberg, Berg) should have been born. In the realm of politics the sense of fragmentation acted no less as a challenge. The more the "whole," the center, the old loyalties were questioned by the increasingly centrifugal nationalisms, the more did the specific Habsburg mission in Central Europe give way to the general task of combining supranational organization with a spirit of freedom and tolerance. In this sense the Habsburg experiment, now a closed chapter in history, leaves twentieth-century man with some important lessons, and it is safe to reiterate Bahr's assertion that Austria was necessary for the world.

In presenting the history of the House of Habsburg to the American reader there is a distinct element of historical delicacy. The stock of the Habsburgs through most of the nineteenth century has been decidedly low in the United States.[2] Austria was not merely far away; the New World saw the old Catholic monarchy as "that monstrous medieval thing." The revolutionary events of 1848–49 in the Austrian Empire were particularly disturbing to Americans who sympathized with the struggle against what Charles Sumner called "patriarchial despotism." What an irony that the New York *Tribune*, comparing the sieges of Vienna in 1848 and 1683, should have likened the revolutionary Viennese of 1848 to the Christian defenders of the city in 1683, and the imbecile Emperor to the Turks![3] The Kossuth craze which swept the county in 1849 fully prejudiced Americans against Austria. Representative of this mood was Elizabeth Peabody, one of

---

[2] For excellent material on this problem see John Gerow Gazley, *American Opinion of German Unification, 1848–1871*, New York, 1926. See also Friedrich Engel-Janosi, " 'Détruisez l'Autriche-Hongrie!' " in *Spectrum Austriae*, ed. by Otto Schulmeister, Vienna, 1957, pp. 241 ff.

[3] Gazley, *American Opinion*, pp. 36 f.

the three Peabody sisters of Salem, who in 1852 came out
with her strange little volume of spiced "extracts" entitled
Crimes of the House of Austria against Mankind: "Its whole
conduct from Rodolph downwards, with reference not merely
to Hungary, but to every nation and province of a nation,
with which it has come into contact, demonstrates, that it is
an enemy to all international law which deserves the name
of Public Right."[4] The image of the Habsburgs that prevailed
in the United States was therefore, like the one created by
the European Whig historian, distinctly negative and it in
turn determined the positive American attitudes toward the
nineteenth-century freedom movements, including Italian
and German unification.

Meanwhile a dissenting assessment of Austria emerged, not
only from American Catholics, but also from American diplomatic reports from Vienna. The historian-diplomat John
Lothrop Motley sent home reports that showed a more sober
evaluation of Austria's role in European politics as well as
an acute awareness of the similarity between Austria's and
America's tasks: "The problem of how to create a nation out
of nationalities . . . an empire out of provinces and states is
as old as history and one of the most difficult and the most
important for human sagacity to solve."[5] During the first
war (1915) the same kind of thought made Hofmannsthal
refer to Austria as "a European America" and suggest whim-
sically that every door leading into Austria carry the inscription "Here or nowhere else is America." But then the war
itself showed up the gulf between the United States and the
Habsburg monarchy. And if the breakup of the monarchy
was not the aim of President Wilson's policy, it was a logical
outcome of his ideological position.

During the Second World War America, which for dec-

---

[4] Elizabeth P. Peabody, *Crimes of the House of Austria against Mankind*,
New York, 1852, pp. 225 f.
[5] Engel-Janosi, " 'Détruisez'," p. 243.

ades had been a haven for the hundreds of thousands of "uprooted" from the monarchy, opened its doors to their first family itself, the Habsburgs.

Since the Second World War Habsburg Austria has no longer appeared as the villain. Ironically, in the eyes of American opinion, historical Austria has exchanged roles with historical Prussia. A new legend has been born of the "good" Austrian and the "bad" Prusso-German in spit of the occurrence in recent history of that infamous "renegade Austrian." Austria is seen nowadays as Hofmannsthal's and Rilke's, Freud's, Schönberg's, Wittgenstein's, Kafka's Austria. Their achievement somehow seems to vindicate Francis Joseph's Austria. The "message" of Kafka's dead "emperor," if Kafka could be thus literally interpreted, has apparently come through after all . . . "you might receive that message as you sit by your window and drowse, while evening falls."

Finally, there is the work of the American historians. Instead of creating legends and counterlegends, they have made the United States an important center for the study of the Habsburg monarchy and its peoples.[6] The position as a world power which the United States has assumed in the twentieth century inevitably invites an analysis of the Habsburg precedent. Moreover, the two World Wars, which have broken out over the struggle for Central Europe, have moved this area dramatically into focus. Central Europe then has ceased to be *terra incognita*, and the path is cleared for a detached assessment of the Habsburg historical role and achievement. May this volume in its English translation contribute to this task.

[6] See for example the work of such scholars as Oscar Jászi, Charles and Barbara Jelavich, Robert A. Kann, Hans Kohn, Arthur J. May, R. John Rath (*Austrian History Yearbook*), Carl Schorske, S. Harrison Thomson (*Journal of Central European Affairs*).

The House of Habsburg

1: The Habsburgs and History

In the summer of 1868, two years after the battle of König-grätz, Leopold von Ranke wrote to Alfred von Arneth that the House, Court, and State Archive in Vienna, which Arneth had just been appointed to direct, was "without any doubt the most important archive for German history."

This verdict of the greatest German historian remains fully valid today. We may even add that the Viennese archive is one of the most important for all European history, since the geographical location and the importance of the German people in Europe ensure that "the most important archive for German history" must belong in the first rank. It is more than just the imperial archive of the Holy Roman Empire, the Emperor, and the chief imperial offices, more also than the archive of a state progressing from the Austrian dukedoms through the growth and maturity of the Austrian hegemony and the Austrian Empire to the Austro-Hungarian monarchy and finally the Austrian Republic. While it is all this, it is primarily, as its ancient and full title of House, Court, and State Archive makes plain, the archives of a "House," a ruling dynasty. According to the reorganization proposed by Rosenthal and approved by the Empress Maria Theresa on September 13, 1749, it contains, "*Privilegia domus augustae, documenta genealogica, pacta familiae, Erbteilungen und Vergleiche, Heiratstractate, Verzichte, Testamente, Vormundschaftsbestellungen und andere acta domus singularia seu domestica*" (Privileges of the august House, genealogical documents, family agreements, allotments of inheritance and settlements, marriage contracts, formal renunciations, wills, appointments of legal guardians, and other particular or domestic acts of the House). And for almost six hundred and fifty years, from the thirteenth to the twentieth century, this august House of the ruling family of Habsburg was one of the leading dynasties, and for most of the time the leading dynasty, in Europe.

No other ruling family was so "European," or became in the course of historical development so much an embodiment and representative of a universal and supranational principle of monarchy. No other European ruling family spread its control over such different European peoples and nations; at the time of its greatest power Charles V, the head of the family, was justly able to make the well-known statement that his was an Empire on which the sun never set. No other ruling family, throughout the centuries until the end of its power, was served by men of so many different European countries: Germans, Dutch, Burgundians, Italians, Spaniards, Frenchmen, Irishmen, Scandinavians, most Slavic peoples, Magyars, Greeks, and Albanians. If one runs over in one's mind the splendid list of generals and chiefs of staff and higher-ranking officers who served and fought under Habsburg banners, or the no less splendid list of statesmen, counselors, and high civil servants, one finds (as was never true for any other state or dynasty) an intermixture of representatives from all European countries, the flower of the European aristocracy, of the European middle class, and of the artistic and academic worlds.

Even today, any visitor to Vienna can be deeply impressed by this harmony of European peoples when he passes the Baroque palaces of the nobility in the center or in the suburbs of the "imperial city," and reflects on their names, those of German, Dutch, Italian, Spanish, French, Hungarian, Bohemain, and Polish aristocracy—Liechtenstein, Auersperg, Kinsky, Harrach, Starhemberg, Palffy, Esterhazy, Collalto, Pallavicini, Clary, Rasumovsky, Clam-Gallas, and so forth. From the end of the thirteenth century, when the Habsburgs brought their Alamannian retainers with them as they left their southwest-German home for Austria, men from each newly acquired country entered their service, and their descendants often remained at court even after their native lands were no longer under Habsburg control.

All these men of diverse nationalities—the Piedmontese Gattinara, chancellor to Charles V; the great Prince Eugene, "Eugenio of Savoy" as he signed himself, uniting two principal European languages in his name; Count Mercy from Lorraine; Bartenstein, son of a Strassburg professor; the Dutchman Van Swieten, court physician, counselor, and general to the Empress Maria Theresa; Laudon from the Baltic; Metternich from the Rhineland; Count Taaffe, scion of an originally Irish family and for many years Prime Minister to the Emperor Francis Joseph—were all "Austrians," because they served the Habsburg "House of Austria" no matter what their nationality. Still other "Austrians" came from the Austrian dependencies on the upper Rhine or in Italy, Holland, or Spain, from the "Empire" of the middle-sized and small German principalities, from the Austrian Alps or Bohemia, Moravia, and Silesia, from Hungary, Poland, or the southern Slavic border regions. The names of officers in the separate regiments listed in the "Schematismus," or rank list of the old royal and imperial army, give the same strong impression of a polyglot community, and even today the astute observer, like the geologist seeing in strata the traces of past ages, can follow in a Viennese address or telephone book the influences left on the Viennese population by the acquisition of Burgundy and Spain, and the ties to northern Italy or to Bohemia and Hungary.

Up to the last engagement in the First World War the Army, which was bound by an entirely personal concept of loyalty to the Habsburg Emperor, was the only European force, in a continent full of nationalist states and national armies, that counted foreigners of the most diverse nationalities among its officers, not in a Foreign Legion, but in a supranational medley which was a last echo of that in Wallenstein's army, and which Schiller portrayed so impressively in his *Wallenstein* trilogy. In the First World War Danish, Swedish, and even French officers served in the Austrian Army and remained loyal to the Emperor throughout, although at the outbreak of war they had been given free permission to return home to their native countries.

A history of the Habsburgs ought therefore to be a history of Europe, and that is the first major difficulty in our way. It is significant that the last detailed history of the family appeared more than a hundred years ago, the great *Geschichte des Hauses Habsburgs* (*History of the House of Habsburg*) by Eduard Maria, Prince Lichnowsky, who was supposed to have been encouraged in the project by Metternich, and that it consists of eight volumes (published from 1836–44) covering only the period from the beginning up to Maximilian I. Its bulk alone is imposing. The book is a result of the flowering of historical science after the "birth of historicism," and it is permeated by the "Christian-Germanic" ideology of the late Romantic period. At the same time it represents a final station in the long series of court-genealogists' histories, running from the late medieval chroniclers and historians Mathias von Neuenburg and Heinrich von Gundelfingen, through Emperor Maximilian I's circle of humanists, Mennel, Cuspinian, Lazius, Sunthaym, and Gerard von Roo. The series continues through the ornamental Baroque historical writing of Guillimann, Gans, Kirchmayer, Eccard, Schönleben, Marquard Herrgott, Beer, and finally through Hormayr's *Oesterreichischen Plutarch* (*Austrian Plutarch*) into the middle of the nineteenth century, thus lasting until the change in historical science brought about by the development and refinement of textual criticism of historical sources.

This change was marked in the Habsburg Empire by the founding, in 1854, of an "Institute of Austrian Historical

Research" which, especially under the direction of Theodor Sickel, carved out a new path for itself. For under the influence of the Sickel school, which concentrated on documentary research, especially relating to the High Middle Ages (and indeed also because of the more and more clearly emerging internal problems of the Habsburg Empire, whose creation and theories of rule were felt to be in opposition to "the trends of the times"), serious Austrian scholarship in the second half of the nineteenth century did not exactly abandon the history of the Empire and the dynasty, but left it chiefly to be delineated in breadth by popular-patriotic literature. It may also be symptomatic that Ottokar Lorenz, one of the most original and interesting, though also most controversial and contradictory, Austrian historians of the second half of the century, who as a young scholar had edited a collection of biographies, *Die Oesterreichische Regentenhalle* (*The Austrian Gallery of Regents*), Vienna, 1857, in tune with the spirit of innovation abroad in the first years of the young Francis Joseph's régime, turned from an admirer to a passionate enemy of the Habsburgs, like Freiherr von Hormayr before him in the first half of the nineteenth century, and, ending as a convinced partisan of the Little-German (*Kleindeutsch*) and Prussian monarchies, left Austria.

A more recent change appeared first around the turn of the century, principally because of the admirable work of Oswald Redlich, under whose editorship the enormous and still incomplete project of the *Regesta Habsburgica* (*Habsburg Digest*) was undertaken. This entailed the publication of all the official Habsburg documents in digest form, which impressively revealed the vast, almost all-European scope of interests among even the early Habsburgs. In numerous specialized publications, starting with his essay on "Die Anfänge Rudolfs I" ("Rudolf I's Beginnings") which appeared in 1889, Redlich concentrated on the history of the first Habsburgs on the German throne. Finally, with his monumental work, *Rudolf von Habsburg, Das Deutsche Reich nach dem Untergang des alten Kaiserreiches* (*Rudolf of Habsburg, the German Kingdom after the End of the Old Empire*), he completed a major history that at last rested on the solid and secure basis of critical study of the sources. Redlich's new approach was certainly also a sign that the great Habsburg crisis of 1866–67, which reached its climax in the loss of the German and Italian possessions and the "compensation" with Hungary, had been overcome and intellectually digested by the turn of the century, and that belief in the vital powers of the Habsburg league of states was growing stronger again.

Redlich's work, which also included the history of King Rudolf's Habsburg predecessors, indicated a new departure in historical writing about the House. In the last fifty years innumerable specialized research projects, biographies of individual rulers, and studies of single periods, have appeared, as well as larger and more inclusive works on Austrian history. The end of Habsburg rule in 1918 did not in the least dampen, but rather stimulated, interest in research and historical writing about the Habsburgs. Nothing on Lichnowsky's scale has since been tried, and it is probable that the swollen flood of specialist publications alone renders a similar attempt beyond the powers of any one scholar. The amount of literature available on the different periods and rulers is also highly variable. Outstanding publications, measuring up to the newest standards of scholarship, exist on individual rulers—to mention only the awe-inspiring two volumes by Karl Brandi on Charles V—while for others, like Frederick III, the pioneer work is still to be done. A broadly depicted and wide-ranging account of the House of Austria would largely coincide with existing histories of Austria—above all with Hugo Hantsch's two volumes—though it would not completely duplicate them. It would take account of a wider field: the older Habsburgs before Rudolf I, the Spanish Habsburgs, and the cadet lines in Italy, but by omitting the Babenberger period and everything that did not deal directly with the history of the House, it would be more narrowly restricted. Above all it would be clearly distinguished from Austrian histories by its choice of point of view and its judgments and evaluations.

The same is true of the present attempt to portray in broad outline the fate of this exalted dynasty, so important in European history. In so doing the concept of the House and the family itself must obviously take the center of the stage. Some difficulties and problems arising from this approach must be mentioned.

Every family and every ruling dynasty is a biological community, whose members can be recognized by outsiders through certain common hereditary qualities of body, mind, and character. At the same time, however—and this is particularly true for dynasties—it is a society of traditions, in which recollections, family myths, and legends develop a certain power to bind and almost to bewitch even members that have married into it. Since it is difficult to distinguish neatly the individual components in the appearance and personality of a man from a middle-class family (as Goethe half-seriously and half-jokingly tried to do for himself in the much-quoted, "Vom Vater hab' ich die Statur . . ." [From my father I got my build . . .]), it is particularly difficult with a European ruling family like that of the Habsburgs, who very early and not without justice considered that they united "all the noble blood" of Europe in their family tree and, on the other hand, that they had contributed their blood to nearly all the other European ruling families. It is extremely problematical to try to define the hereditary qualities added to the Habsburg family tree by a particular marriage, or to follow the Habsburg traces in other ruling families. Certainly external characteristics like the well-known Habsburg nose and Habsburg lower lip were inherited down the centuries with astonishing persistency, and finally through the inbreeding of the Spanish Habsburgs degenerated into the grotesque. Also it is frequently tempting to compare personalities even when they are generations apart, and to establish the illuminating reappearance of particular qualities (which occur according to genetic laws), such as the incontestable similarity between Frederick III and Francis I, Joseph I and Joseph II, and others.

Finally it may be tempting to try to extract two or three "prototypes" from the long series of Habsburg figures and to follow them from the family's beginnings up to our century. Such figures are the aggressive ruler, the bold planner, repeatedly wrecking his ambitions and large-scale plans against reality (Rudolf IV, "the Founder"; Maximilian I; Joseph II; and perhaps also Maximilian of Mexico and Francis Ferdinand); the contrasting hesitant and doggedly conservative ruler, seeking security in rigidity and often finding it (Frederick III, Rudolf II, Leopold I, Francis I); finally, the mean between these two types of ruler, who, either through a fortunate disposition or else through a long lifetime of experience, seem to have maintained a certain balance between the tendencies to boldness and caution, between reform of the outworn and preservation of the valuable (Rudolf I, Ferdinand I, Maria Theresa, Francis Joseph I). But apart from the exaggeration of likenesses and blurring of individual differences that every such effort to classify and type necessarily involves, the result would be simply to establish basic types of ruler (or, in fact, of all those politically active and responsible), which obviously also occurred among the Habsburgs.

The frequent appearance in Habsburg history of extremely dissimilar brothers (Frederick the Handsome and his brothers, Rudolf the Founder and his brothers, Frederick III and Albert VI—the sons of Ernest the Iron Duke, Charles V and Ferdinand I, Rudolf II and Matthias, Joseph I and Charles VI, Joseph II and Leopold II, Francis I and his brothers, Francis Joseph I and his brothers) suggests the need for caution. Not even the use of modern biological laws of genetics explains everything. Court historians in the early centuries searched for and praised the perpetuation of all virtues and noble qualities from the "illustrious Ancestor" Rudolf (or from his forebears as far back as the Romans, Trojans, and biblical ancestors of mankind) through their inheritance by all the subsequent generations of Habsburgs. Later, however, it became fashionable to see in a family that up to the present day has produced a series of men remarkable for character and intellect only a textbook illustration of the transmission of psychological illnesses, insanity, neurotic suspicion, and pathological depression, and to draw a bold line from mad Joanna through Don Carlos and Rudolf II, the evident symptoms of degeneracy among the later Spanish Habsburgs and also Charles VI, up to the mental incapacity of Francis Joseph's uncle and predecessor Ferdinand I, and the tragedy of Crown Prince Rudolf. This way of looking at things is exactly as one-sided and therefore distorting as that of the earlier court historians and panegyrists.

A purely genealogical and biological point of view cannot do justice to such an important part of European history as the House of Habsburg; it must be amplified and extended by the view of the ruling family as a society of traditions, within which the transmitted accounts of ancestral deeds, achievements, mistakes, blunders, and strokes of good and bad luck possessed a powerful ability to mold character and behavior.

To see almost a thousand years of Habsburg history in terms of the House, or family, suits the subject itself and is the most profitable point of view. This concept was central to the plans, wishes, and actions of the Habsburg rulers at least until well into the eighteenth century. In the following hundred and fifty years ideas of duty—to the family, the family tradition, the head of the family, and the family laws —still played a decisive role, along with others by no means so strange to the early rulers as is commonly supposed—ideas of the welfare of the state and of its subjects. The first determined effort to establish a permanent hereditary monarchy—which, as now appears, could have led to the development of a strong German monarchy like that of the French and the English—was cut off by a bloody family tragedy, the murder of King Albert I by his nephew John and his fellow conspirators, as a result of a quarrel over House and family law. In the same way, the end of Habsburg-Lorraine sovereignty was preceded by the well-known family conflicts between individual members of the Arch-house who rejected the family statutes and the head of the family who embodied the severity of this patriarchal system. The last Habsburg Emperor answered in plain human terms the question put to him in exile about his reasons for leaving Austria of his own free will, "he did it, though it was perhaps a political error, for the sake of his children, whom he considered to be threatened." It was an answer that, quite unintentionally, fitted neatly into the tradition of a family that had as its most important and attractive figure the motherly Maria Theresa, and that, even when it was unfashionable in the ruling families of Europe, was marked by a model family life and strong family solidarity. Similarly, the whole business of mistresses and extra-marital affairs plays a much smaller part in Habsburg history than in the history of most other European ruling houses.

Certainly the idea of "House"—of family sovereignty, power, prestige, and wealth—was not the only motive power in Habsburg history. Rule over Austria, the country whose name attached itself to that of the family in the title "Casa d' Austria," or House of Austria, became in the course of centuries increasingly the formative and determining element in Habsburg policies. Possession of the German crown, the crown of the Holy Roman Empire, which finally became a sort of customary privilege, sheds on the family from Rudolf

I onward (German history includes twenty Habsburg emperors or kings) the glory of the highest consecration, and was eminently important in arousing and strengthening the deep conviction among the Habsburgs and their subjects of the family's election and majesty, and its vocation for the highest position of sovereignty in Christendom. An expert opinion of Ferdinand II's council says,

> When one considers from what source Upper and Lower, Outer and Inner Austrian lands, the Kingdoms of Hungary and Bohemia, the County of Milan and many other estimable lands come to this most praiseworthy House, it will be evident that, although *matrimonia* has contributed, yet *principaliter* these noble *accessiones* have come pouring in from the Roman Empire and the Roman Kingdom, and have been protected against all *nemicos* and their *machinationes* not less by imperial authority than by their own strength and the strength of the various lands.

Almost a hundred and fifty years later Count Johann Anton Pergen emphasized in a memorandum which he had drawn up at Joseph II's request, that

> there are most important reasons extant, which can convincingly establish that the imperial crown was the original source of the flourishing and continuance of the Serene Arch-House, that it has provided support until this day for its greatness, power, and dignity, and the preservation of the same has become absolutely needful; history teaches every man that the power of the Serene Arch-House has grown gradually, and shows that the ornament of the imperial crown has strengthened it from age to age.

In the domains that fell to them through election, inheritance, marriage, or the spoils of war, the Habsburgs always made an effort to adapt themselves to the customs of the country, to learn its language, and to attract its nobility into their service and to their court; in this way they partly assimilated the nationality of their subject nations and peoples. The "German" Maximilian I, the "Burgundian" Charles V, the "Spanish" Philip II, the "Tyrolean," "Styrian," and

"Hungarian" Archdukes, the members of the "Italian" cadet lines certainly felt themselves to be, some more and some less, "native sons" of these countries and, in a broader sense, members of their particular peoples, though above all members of a supranational House that was exalted above its subject dominions. Even in the period of fully developed "integral" nationalism the Habsburgs succeeded in conveying this feeling of standing above the nations to the whole category of "servants" of the imperial House, to the members of the bureaucracy and the army.

For this reason, any history of the Habsburg successes and failures that regards them from the point of view of only one country or a group of countries—such as the Danubian monarchy from 1867 to 1918—or measures them by national standards, must necessarily be one-sided. Though the importance of Habsburg history for German history (and vice-versa) can hardly be ignored, and though it may be legitimate for the writer of a history of the German people to measure Habsburg success and failure according to these standards, the point of view is scarcely adequate for an attempt to relate the history of the House itself. This is evident even in such a worthwhile collection as Gustav Roloff's *Das Habsburger-Reich, von seiner Entstehung bis zu seinem Untergang* (*The Rise and Fall of the Habsburg Empire*), Sammlung Göschen, Berlin, 1936, or in the extreme and polemical distortion of Alfred Rapp's book, published in the same year, *Die Habsburger, Die Tragödie eines halben Jahrtausends deutscher Geschichte*, (*The Habsburgs, the Tragedy of Five Hundred Years of German History*). Since German and Habsburg history present two large groups of subject matter that largely overlap but do not completely coincide, the treatment of each demands a different point of view and, accordingly, a different evaluation. If this is not done, the historian is inevitably enmeshed in a net of superficial judgments on "un-Germanic dynastic policies," judgments that can without difficulty be matched by the opposing objections of Italian, Hungarian, or Slavic historians to the far too "Germanic policies" of the same family. If one wishes to approach more closely to the historical phenomenon of the House of Habsburg and to understand—if not the final causes that remain secret from even the most Argus-eyed and conscientious historian—at least the prerequisites and conditions for the rise and centuries-long flowering of this ruling dynasty and for its gain and loss of lands and sovereignties, then one must always try to find out how the Habsburgs themselves regarded their own history, or how they wished it to be regarded by others, not only by subjects and friends, but also by opponents and enemies. The broad field of genealogical legend and theories of descent can no more be neglected than those subjects hardly touched on as yet: Habsburg piety, the royal way of life, and the principles followed in the education of future rulers. Thus one returns to the [already-mentioned] concept of the ruling family as a society of traditions, a sequence of generations that, over and above the blood relationship, is bound together by a common tradition, not remaining static through the course of centuries but always changing, taking on new elements and rejecting old. The development of this tradition, and its contest with contemporary political facts, the constellations of European political power, and the great contemporary movements in different periods and centuries is the proper theme of the present study.

2: Romans, Trojans, or Alamanni?

There is a story that once, when the argument among the genealogists about the "*origines serenissimae ac potentissimae Domus Habsburge-Austriacae*" (the origins of the Hapsburg Arch-House) had broken out again with particular violence, Emperor Ferdinand II exclaimed petulantly that, if these gentlemen were to exert themselves any more diligently in pursuit of the origins of his forebears, he feared they would in the end come up with shepherds. Since similar utterances are reported of other Habsburgs, both earlier and later, it is clear that, though convinced their House had been specially chosen for a particular mission, they nevertheless remained conscious of the kinship of all men, "the common descent from Adam."

Yet the endeavors to investigate the origins of the Habsburgs, to trace their lineage back through Roman patrician families to Julius Caesar and from him through Aeneas to the Trojans, or through the Carolingians and Merovingians and thence by way of the Frankish genealogical legends directly to the Trojans, or even through Osiris and Jupiter to Cham and Noah, cannot be simply dismissed as abstruse and idle games played by pseudo-learned and reward-hungry genealogists and court-historiographers. For in the controversy—lasting well over six centuries and involving the scholars and writers of almost all European nations—one can recognize both an echo of the importance of the House and traces of its real political aspirations, claims, and large-scale designs.

The attempts to emphasize the aristocratic and royal descent of the House, and to support the theory with genealogical legends, tales, pseudo-learned fabrications, and family trees, started therefore at the end of the thirteenth century, just when Rudolf of Habsburg, the first of his House to attain European stature and the ancestor of Habsburg world power, established the family for the first time on the German throne. To counteract the propaganda of the enemies of the Habsburgs, who spread about the legend of the "poor Count," his noble lineage had to be emphasized. Claiming descent from the Hohenstaufens or Salians was impossible, and, moreover, since it was necessary to maintain good relations with the Pope, would have been politically inexpedient. What seemed to historians of the nineteenth and twentieth centuries to be the most impressive point, the ideological and political union between the Habsburgs and the Hohenstaufens, the *"translatio Imperii,"* or continuation of the Empire beyond the interregnum (exemplified by the faithful service rendered to the Hohenstaufens by Rudolf, his father, and grandfather, and—of even greater symbolic force—the fact that Rudolf had been lifted from the font by the last great Emperor of the High Middle Ages, the mighty Frederick II himself), could not count in the eyes of contemporaries as an effective argument to support the Habsburg claims to royal or imperial office.

Therefore, around the beginning of the fourteenth century, and probably among the lowland Swiss followers of the first royal Habsburgs, the legend arose that the Habsburgs were descended from a Roman patrician family, the Colonna, who in turn traced their ancestry through the Counts of Tusculum to the *gens Julia* and thus to Julius Caesar. In the fourteenth and part of the fifteenth century the Habsburgs believed in this genealogy. Even in times when the possibility of regaining the throne did not seem imminent, they saw in it support for their unchanging belief in the royal destiny of their family. Like the particular form assumed by the idea of Rome and the *renovatio*-myth (belief in the revival of the

Roman Empire) after Dante and after the fall of the Hohenstaufens, the theory suited humanistic learning and modes of thought in the late Middle Ages. At the same time, it was also adapted to the attitude taken by the Popes (and by the Roman nobility dominating the Papacy) to the candidates for the German throne after the interregnum, and particularly to the Habsburgs.

But in the fifteenth century (at a time when other less important families—such as the Tyrolean lords of Völs or Matsch, and finally even the Hohenzollerns—also claimed descent from the Colonna) there arose along with the Colonna legend a theory that the Habsburgs sprang from another Roman patrician family, the Pierleoni, the "Counts of Aventine," and before them from the ancient Roman Anicii. This theory, which appeared for the first time around 1476, was advanced particularly to indicate the "holiness of the Habsburgs" (Popes Felix III [492–96] and Gregory I or the Great [590–604], as well as St. Benedict, the founder of western monasticism, were descended from the Anicii), and especially during the Counter Reformation it was stubbornly maintained by its champions, the Pierleonists, against the adherents of the Frankish-Trojan theory of ancestry. It is almost certainly no accident that this hypothesis of Roman descent appeared anew in a period when the Papacy, revivified by Catholic reforms, had again become more influential politically and intellectually. Around the middle of the seventeenth century, when Rome's newly increased importance in European politics had again diminished, scholars concluded that the Pierleoni had originally been Jews from the medieval Roman ghetto. Thereupon the Pierleoni thesis, originally advanced by Heinrich von Gundelfingen in the fifteenth century, was dropped, to be briefly revived in the middle of the twentieth century by the National Socialists to defame the hated dynasty on the grounds of its "non-Aryan descent."

Side by side with the Roman theory soon appeared the

Frankish, whose relevance to political aspirations is equally evident. It traced the descent of the Habsburgs from the Franks (occasionally from the Carolingians, but usually through the legitimate dynasty of the Merovingians) directly to the Trojans, thus bypassing the Romans entirely. The propagation of this thesis was often accompanied by unmistakable signs of anti-Roman and anti-Italian prejudice. Where the Roman theory focused on the south, on Rome, "*Urbs aeterna*" and the "capital of the world," the Franco-Trojan theory anticipated union with the west, and the effort of the Habsburgs to legitimize themselves, in opposition to the French royal House, as the true heirs of the Carolingian and Merovingian realm. Not unexpectedly, the most outspoken promulgator and advocate of the Frankish theory was Maximilian I, who, through his marriage with Mary of Burgundy, started the new westward trend of his House and, as heir of the Dukes of Burgundy, also inherited the Burgundian conflict with the French. Certainly Maximilian was moved by other considerations as well. Of all the Habsburgs he occupied himself most intensively with the genealogy of his House; he inspired and sponsored numerous works on the subject and sought to immortalize it artistically in illuminated manuscripts, books on heraldry, pictorial family trees, and finally in the grandiose but only partly completed program for his tomb. Standing at the turning point between medieval and modern times, between Gothic and Renaissance, he unified in his own person the separate branches of his House, thereby inheriting their widely divergent political aspirations and traditions. The ruler who succeeded in securing Burgundy and Spain for his House, who prepared for the acquisition of Hungary and Bohemia, and even played with the idea of setting the papal tiara on his own head, whose bold fantasy and cautious political realism were so firmly, attractively, and inextricably intertwined, revealed in his genealogical interests the most varied of impulses. The already mentioned anti-Roman and anti-Italian prejudices, in conjunction with nationalistic German leanings, are as recognizable as the turning toward Greek antiquity, the claim to appropriate the intellectual and political inheritance of Byzantium, which was stimulated by humanistic scholarship and historically conscious politics, and which was to be supported specifically by the Frankish-Trojan theory of descent. Equally apparent is the important role that opposition to the French kingdom, which found expression again and again in their genealogical preoccupations, played for Maximilian and his successors.

For almost three centuries—from the Burgundian marriage of 1477 to the Franco-Austrian alliance of 1756—this opposition remained a decisive factor in Habsburg politics. When it was finally replaced by a new hostility between the two great German powers, Austria and Prussia, new political aspirations destroyed the basis for the long-outmoded genealogical speculations just as historical scholarship had done long before. Yet an important remnant was left, which could be brought into play in the new struggle for hegemony in Germany, extending for over a century. This was the theory of Habsburg descent from the Etichoni, Alamannian dukes in Swabia and Alsace, who were then supposed to be ancestors common to both Habsburgs and Lotharingians. It was first advanced in 1649 by the Frenchman Jérome Vignier, who posited a common descent of Habsburgs and Lotharingians from a "House of Alsace," which he traced back in turn to a certain Archinoald, mayor of the palace to Clovis II.

In 1721 the Hanoverian librarian, Johann Georg Eccard, traced Eticho back to the Alamannian dukes. Finally, Marquard Herrgott (1694–1762), a learned monk of St. Blasien, who had been commissioned by the last male Habsburg of the old line, the Emperor Charles V, to produce his great work on Habsburg family history, emphatically proclaimed Eticho to be the common ancestor of Habsburgs and Lotharingians. The work, carried out with seventeenth- and eight-eenth-century methods of evaluating source materials, was based principally on the *Acta Murensia,* the annals of the monastery of Muri in the Aargau (a Habsburg foundation), which date back to the twelfth century and which became known in 1618. The result of these investigations coincided with both the dynastic and the political ambitions of the Habsburgs in the eighteenth and nineteenth centuries. When the last female Habsburg, Maria Theresa, united two fami-lies by marrying Francis Stephen of Lorraine, the theory of kinship with the Lotharingian ducal house, derived from their common descent from the Etichoni, bestowed on the new House of Habsburg-Lorraine the blessing of historical tradition and divine predestination.

But descent from the old Alamannic ducal dynasty, accord-ing to the fashionable "Christian-Germanic" ideology and the romantic nineteenth-century doctrine of the national soul, made the Habsburgs peculiarly suited as legitimate rulers in Germany. The legendary holy forebears—St. Morandus, re-vered as a Habsburg ancestor in the late Middle Ages, as well as the saints of the Pierleoni family, and the legendary "Habs-burg Ottobert, Count of Altenburg," celebrated in the Ba-roque period—succumbed to the critical rationalism of the day; the numerous Baroque cults of saints and their feast days vanished in the flood of the Enlightenment and of *Josephinismus.*[1] Only the legendary "Duke Eticho," or "Count Eticho," remained on the leafless Habsburg family tree, stripped of its saints and primal ancestors, of its Ger-manic, classical, and biblical kings and heroes. On the ceil-ing of one of the rooms in Castle Laxenburg near Vienna (a romantic version of a "medieval German knights' castle" built by Francis, the last Roman and first Austrian emperor),

[1] A term commonly used by German historians to designate the spirit and atmosphere of the age of Emperor Joseph II, as discussed in Chapter 13.

Eticho, together with the royal (and real) ancestor Rudolf, leads off the procession of the great forebears.

In 1836 Prince Lichnowsky, the last in the line of Habsburg court-historiographers to treat this subject, put a final period to the genealogical elaborations of his predecessors. He wrote,

> When this dynasty ascended the most important thrones of the world, many searched for its antecedents among the most famous races and nations, as if the generally recognized nobility of the House were not enough. For there was never a family resplendent with wealth or power whose origin was not traced back to the remotest past by avaricious genealogists and historiographers.

He berated the medieval historian for "impudently, and in contempt of all historical probability, [finding] among the Julii and Scipioni or Anicii, or even the barely known Aventine Pierleoni, the willing progenitor of the prince who rewarded and sustained him," while others, not satisfied even with this, went "back to Hector, yes, even to Japhet, enumerating the names in detailed sequence, as if the history of the remotest millennia were spread out before them like a contemporary chronicle."

After alluding to the contemporary example of Napoleon, who found himself genealogists "that wanted to make the Corsican son of the revolution into a descendant of the oldest families of the Eternal City or the aborigines of Italy," Lichnowsky drew the final conclusion,

> For the conscientious historian this much may suffice: if in the tenth and eleventh centuries a family already was demonstrably numbered among those in positions of command and high esteem, then it must be counted as belonging to the highest nobility, and one can be sure that its progenitor in the preceding centuries was among those surrounding the Carolingian throne, and that he must have been equal in rank to the granddaughters of the mayors of the palace and their relatives. Anything more is superfluous; the man was eminently noble, and this indeed can suffice.

Here the attempt is still being made, one might almost say diffidently, to trace the origins of the ruling dynasty, as a family among "those in positions of command and high esteem," back to the Carolingian epoch and thus to the beginnings of German history. Yet half a century later—during the flowering of scientific positivism, and after the foundation of the Hohenzollern Empire had settled history's rejection of the Habsburg claim to leadership in Germany—Franz Ritter von Krones, in his *Grundriss der österreichischen Geschichte* (*Outline of Austrian History*), Vienna, 1889, pp. 302 ff., dropped even this hypothesis, though it is eminently justifiable and, at least up to the present day, has not been proved demonstrably false. Introducing his first attempt at a critical survey of the genealogical legends as literary history, Krones stated firmly,

> The cradle of the Habsburgs lay in Alamannian Switzerland; the family name and historical reputation hark back to the eleventh century. . . . The Habsburg rise to power after the thirteenth century, especially as the House took over the German royal crown and grew steadily richer in land, entailed—as it did for all other great princely Houses—an abundance of genealogical brown studies, often as artificial as they were insignificant, which lost themselves in the dimmest twilight of prehistory.

This point of view has been shared by all other serious scholars. As Alphons Lhotsky established in his pioneering study *Apis Colonna, Fabeln und Theorien über die Abkunft der Habsburger* (*Apis Colonna, Legends and Theories about the Descent of the Habsburgs*), modern research "has refused to undertake any close study of the artificial theories of descent." But very properly he continued,

> Nevertheless these seem to be worth closer observation simply for their own sake, not because the muddied stream of confused borrowings from poetical and historical works, or the not always brilliant inventions and frequent miraculous misunderstandings, yield any hope of an increase in our knowledge of truth, but because of

the significant promptings they gave to artists and works of art. Even the attitude and decisions of the Habsburg rulers may often have been determined by their careful attention to the then-accepted version of their genealogical legend. Views of this kind, expounded by the princes' tutors, shared and at times also refurbished by the most influential counselors, cannot remain irrelevant to the history of art or historical research.

Studies that have appeared since—particularly Anna Coreth's work on the dynastic and political ideas of Emperor Maximilian I—have demonstrated that Lhotsky's point of view was both accurate and most stimulating to scholarship.

But a further observation is unavoidable. The attempts to prove, by means of dynastic legends, that the Habsburgs were predestined to sovereignty and an exceptionally high position accompanied the political plans and acts of the House from its first king, Rudolf, through its golden age under Maximilian to Maria Theresa, last of the old Habsburg line. Even thereafter, under Habsburg-Lorraine, an echo is still detectable, though weakened by the overpowering influence of Enlightenment and Rationalism that determined the intellectual outlook of the members of the House after Joseph II. Francis Ferdinand, the heir to the throne whose assassination at Sarajevo in the summer of 1914 brought about the First World War and with it the end of the Habsburg monarchy, also concerned himself deeply with questions of genealogy, though he strove, in conscious opposition to Joseph's tradition, to revive a religious and metaphysical concept of sovereignty and of the mission and special election of the House of Habsburg.

It is no accident that Maximilian I, creator of Habsburg world power and heir to the widely diversified aspirations of the various branches of the family that were reunited for the first time in him, occupied himself more intensively than any other Habsburg with genealogical theories and legends. It is even less of an accident that, under the influence of Rationalism and Enlightenment, which stimulated the critical writing of history and the critical investigation of historical sources, the heavenful of Habsburg ancestors became more and more depopulated, while at the same time and under the same influence the concepts of the divine right of kings and the sacred nature of the crown, which were engaged in a losing battle with the ideas of the fatherland, the state, and finally the rule of the people, paled more and more.

3: At the Crossroads of the West

Habsburg family history begins with a problem that has not been entirely solved to this day: whether or not "Guntram the Rich," who is considered the ancestor of the dynasty and who must have lived about the middle of the tenth century, is the same as that other Guntram, Count of the Alsatian North province, who was deprived of his possessions for treason in 952 (three years before the battle of the Lechfeld) by Otto I, the great Saxon Emperor and later reviver of the Holy Roman Empire. Certainly a great part of the holdings confiscated from Count Guntram of the North province can later be traced as Habsburg property, which could be explained if either Guntram himself or his descendants were pardoned and had their properties returned to them. The so-called *Eigen* (Original fief), the territory at the confluence of the Aare and Reuss rivers in the present Swiss canton of Aargau, where the "Habsburg" (*Habichtsburg*—hawk's castle) was constructed in 1020, giving the family its name, might have remained in Guntram's possession since it lay in Burgundy, outside the Ottonian Empire. It is also conceivable that this *Eigen* was acquired through marriage. Guntram's son (in one tradition the "Count of Altenburg") was called Lanzelin, the pet name for Landolt; this name occurs in a Thurgau family which formerly held property in the same district on the Aare. If Guntram the Rich was the same as the Count Guntram punished by Otto I, then the Habsburgs are in fact descended from the dukes of Alsace, the Etichoni. The identification of the two Guntrams has, incidentally, been made not only in a pro-Habsburg sense (in order to prove descent from the old Alsatian ducal family and thus from the Lotharingians and Merovingians), but also in recent times by passionate anti-Habsburgs who wished to see in the descent from the "arch-traitor" Guntram an omen for a whole tradition of Habsburg "treason against the people," down to the Sixtus-letter affair[1] in the First World War.

Certainly when we reach the undoubted, as distinct from the supposititious, ancestors of King Rudolf I, they already hold notable rank and property (even the nickname "the Rich" indicates this, since at that time it referred only to landed possessions) in Alsace as well as on the other side of the Rhine in Breisgau, and also in the "upper lands" in the Aargau. Thus from the very beginning of their history the Habsburgs were established in the territory of the erstwhile "middle kingdom" of Lotharingia, in the heart of Europe and of medieval Christendom, the vital European center on the upper course of the Rhine and the passes across the Alps, an area where then, as in later epochs, all political, intellectual, and cultural currents mingled, the crossroads of Europe. From here, as if spontaneously, emerged those numerous connections with the ruling families of Germany, Burgundy, France, and northern Italy that were soon to be found among the Habsburgs.

One of Lanzelin's sons, Radbot, married the Duke of Lorraine's daughter Ita; therefore—without counting the doubtful genesis from Guntram—the Habsburgs are indeed descended from the dukes of Lorraine and are related to the dukes of Swabia as well as to the Capetian kings of France. Another of Lanzelin's sons, Rudolf, married a certain Kunigunde, who probably belonged to the Zollern family. Though we know nothing definite about Lanzelin's eldest son, who bore his father's name, the likely conjecture has been made that one of his daughters married Count Berthold of Villin-

---

[1] The letter of March 24, 1917, in which the Emperor Charles, in secret peace negotiations with Britain and France, wrote he willingly would recognize the "just demand" of the latter to Alsace-Lorraine.

gen and thereby became the ancestress of the dukes of Zähringen. In any case, even in the first generation of which we know more than mere names, the Habsburgs were closely related to the leading families on the Upper Rhine.

The most significant figure in this generation, at the beginning of the eleventh century, was probably Bishop Werner of Strassburg. According to a tradition accepted by nearly all genealogists and historians until the beginning of this century, he too was a son of the elder Lanzelin. But another tradition, which seems well supported, maintains that he was a brother of Ita of Lorraine, and therefore not a Habsburg but a Lotharingian. At all events he is significant in Habsburg family history because, as a boyhood friend of Emperor Henry II and an eager advocate of his election to the throne, he played a considerable part in the further development of Habsburg power. If Guntram the Rich was the count punished by Otto I, then possibly it was Bishop Werner who obtained from Henry II the pardon for Guntram's grandsons —this squares better with the theory that he was the brother-in-law rather than the brother of Count Radbot.

Bishop Werner was a proponent of the policy of expansion into Burgundy, in which the interests of his imperial friend and of the Empire evidently coincided with those of the Habsburgs. It was in connection with the Burgundian wars that the family castle, the Habsburg, was constructed, about 1020, in the Habsburg *Eigen* on the Burgundian border.

There is a legend associated with the building of this castle which, apart from the often self-contradictory theories of ancestry treated in the previous chapter, may be regarded as the oldest of the Habsburg didactic tales. Throughout the centuries these formed a sort of family treasure of pragmatic and pedagogical material with which to educate future rulers, instruct other members of the family, and—last but not least —win and hold the sympathies of subjects, allies, and contemporary public opinion. The legend relates that Count

Radbot built the castle without ramparts, curtain walls, or defensive towers, and was upbraided therefore by the warlike Bishop Werner. Radbot then promised to surround the castle with strong fortifications in one night. The next morning he pointed from a window to the host of his men drawn up around the castle; in their midst the mailclad horsemen loomed up at regular intervals like towers on a wall.

> *Then spake the bishop: "Verily*
> *Keep to such walls, and well for thee!*
> *Naught is so sure*
> *As troth that will for aye endure.*
> *May living walls, its tower of strength,*
> *Guard Habsburg now for centuries' length!*
> *The sight inspires*
> *With joyful awe the German shires,*[2]

according to the poem written by Karl Simrock for a nineteenth-century primer.

Scholarship has established that this legend is migratory, having been related also of the Emperor Frederick I and the Landgrave of Thuringia. It was probably attached to the Habsburgs because of the visual impression made by the castle's high rectangular keep, with living quarters added later. And, as far as we can tell, the link was made at a time when the Habsburg party in its ancestral lands on the Upper Rhine, as well as in the whole Empire, was involved in an extremely bitter fight with the anti-Habsburg party. In its oldest form (as transmitted by Mathias von Neuenburg), the legend treats not of Radbot and Werner, but of a legendary pair of ancestors, brothers who crossed the Alps from Rome. For the Habsburg princes it exemplified the fact that rulers are best protected by the loyalty and affection of their subjects. Faithful to this maxim, a remarkably large number of

[2] An attempt has been made to recapture as faithfully as possible the original doggerel.—Trs.

Habsburg rulers—from Rudolf I down to the Habsburg-Lotharingians—strove successfully, in spite of their sense of majesty, election, and separation from the commonalty, to capture the affection of their subjects and to become truly popular.

The significant position of the family in its ancestral lands on both sides of the Upper Rhine (Alsace, Breisgau, and part of present-day Switzerland) is also demonstrated by the monastic foundations made by Lanzelin's sons in the first half of the eleventh century. About the time the Habsburg was built, Radbot and Ita, possibly also under the influence of Bishop Werner, founded the Benedictine monastery of Muri in the Aargau, which became the family monastery and thus the repository of the oldest and most important records of the family's early history. During the investiture struggle and the monastic reform movement it became, under Radbot and Ita's son Werner, one of the strongholds of the Cluniac and Hirsau reforms.

Radbot's brother Rudolf founded the nunnery of Othmarsheim in the Habsburgs' Alsatian domain, near the Rhine and at the eastern edge of the Hardt forest. Because the church of Othmarsheim is reminiscent of Charlemagne's chapel in Aachen, which by adapting Byzantine forms became for its own time a visible expression of the claim to sovereignty, it illustrates the family's importance and self-confidence even at the beginning of the eleventh century.

The following two centuries brought a slow but steady increase of property and seignoral rights. Later in the eleventh century the Benedictine nunnery of Hermetswyl was founded. Radbot's grandson Otto, who in 1090 became the first of the family to be designated Count of Habsburg, took part as a vassal of Emperor Henry V in the campaign against the Hungarian King Koloman. As "Graf Otto de Havichsburg" he was mentioned in an imperial document from

Pressburg, dated September 29, 1108—the first historically recorded sojourn of a Habsburg in the Danube area.

In the course of the twelfth century the Habsburgs and the Hohenstaufens became more and more closely connected; Habsburgs appeared ever more frequently at court and accompanied the Emperors on their campaigns. The heavy death toll paid by the German high nobility on their expeditions into Burgundy, Italy, and finally the Holy Land claimed victims also among the Habsburgs (Count Albert IV, father of King Rudolf I, died on a crusade in the Holy Land), but the family survived. Since it was closely allied to families who were dying out, it inherited their properties and privileges, a process facilitated still further by the good relations between the Habsburgs and the imperial House, and the important services rendered by the Habsburgs, as guardians of the alpine passes, to the last Hohenstaufens. Habsburg possessions in Alsace and Breisgau and those in the "upper lands"—later Switzerland—steadily increased, and a fusion of both domains to form a huge Habsburg territory in southwest Germany seemed distinctly possible.

The Habsburg who first seemed close to achieving it was Count Rudolf II, "the Old." After switching from the Guelph party of Otto to the Ghibelline (Hohenstaufen) party of Philip during the struggle for the throne that followed the double election of 1198, he was one of the great noblemen in southwest Germany who immediately joined young Frederick II on his appearance in Germany. This bond found visible expression when Emperor Frederick stood godfather to Rudolf's grandson, later King Rudolf I. It was politically valuable in the help granted by the great Hohenstaufen to the Count of Habsburg, as a reward for services rendered, in his plans to acquire land and inheritances, notably in the allotment of the Zähringer property. When Rudolf the Old died in 1232, the Habsburgs were second only to the Kiburg dynasty in the "upper lands," and to the Hohenstaufens in Alsace and Breisgau. The wealth and importance of these supposedly "poor Counts" was illustrated when, in 1212, Rudolf the Old raised 1000 of the 3200 marks' bail for the young king Frederick II, payable to the Duke of Lorraine, while the Archbishop of Mainz, the Bishop of Worms, and four temporal lords jointly raised only 700 marks.

Rudolf the Old's grandson, the same Rudolf who was born on May 1, 1218, and lifted from the font by the Emperor Frederick II, became first heir to the Kiburgs, and finally, in the Empire, heir and successor—but in many respects also liquidator—of Hohenstaufen power, designs, and ideas. But before the Habsburg dynasty, in his person, reached the last step of the ascent to the heights of world politics and the uppermost level of European ruling families, the division of inheritance between the sons of Rudolf the Old, Albert IV and Rudolf III, once more retarded the expansion of Habsburg power.

In 1232, immediately after Rudolf the Old died, his sons (the elder of whom, Albert, had already been acting independently in Alsace during his father's lifetime) divided their lands and privileges. Probably unintentionally, this resulted in a complete separation into two dynastic lines, the elder of which subsequently became royal, while the younger was called Laufenburg after its seignoral seat. But when quarrels arose over the division, the brothers submitted to a court of arbitration, which in 1238–39 carried through the final allocation. This fact, as well as the open opposition between the two lines during the final struggle between the Papacy and the Hohenstaufens (when the elder line of Albert and his son Rudolf fought for the Hohenstaufens, and the younger line of Rudolf III and his sons Gottfried and Eberhard for the Papacy), would seem to indicate that personal conflicts were largely responsible for the split. Indeed, soon after the death of Rudolf III in 1249 the two branches were reconciled. King Rudolf I apparently got on well with his cousin

Gottfried during his entire lifetime, although the Laufenburg or "Counts'" branch in subsequent periods must have always found it oppressive to be overshadowed by the superior royal (later ducal or "Austrian") branch.

Because the partition of 1232–39 was not made according to domains, i.e., between the Alsatian property and that of the "upper lands," it is clear that it was not made for administrative or practical reasons (as might have been supposed from the already considerable size, extent, and geographic dispersion of the Habsburg possessions). Both branches received properties and privileges in both areas, and both held in common a few important estates, chief among which was the landgraviate in Alsace, the highest-ranking imperial fief. As most recent research into Habsburg domestic law has stressed, the principle of collective inheritance and investiture with the total holdings—that is, the right of all sons to inherit in common, in contrast to the principle of primogeniture, or inheritance solely by the eldest son—was maintained by the Habsburgs with notable stubbornness. Only in the eighteenth century, with the Pragmatic Sanction established by Charles VI, the last Habsburg of the old line, was the principle of primogeniture carried through. If the Habsburg divisions of inheritance from the eleventh to the seventeenth centuries did not, by and large, lead to a complete fragmentation of the estates, if they sometimes hindered but never completely prevented the formation of large domains, this is explained by the nature of collective inheritance, which, though it divides and distributes, also—by considering the rights of inheritance of the whole House—unifies and maintains. As a matter of fact, most of the divisions were canceled, after a time, by reversion to the only surviving line. Had it not been for the intervention of foreign powers, even the great division in early modern times between the Spanish-Habsburg and German-Habsburg lines doubtless would have been canceled out in the person of the last

Habsburg of the old line, Charles VI, as is shown by the close ties between the courts of Vienna and Madrid lasting into the seventeenth century. The great importance of the "House" concept throughout Habsburg history had a very real basis in the laws of inheritance; similarly, the Habsburgs proved to be the most tenacious guardians of the traditions of the original European aristocracy and its legal thinking in terms of family and clan, as contrasted with the ancient and modern principles of "public law."

Immediately after the court of arbitration had finally established the partition of the estate between the two sons of Rudolf the Old, the elder, Count Albert IV, went on a crusade and died in the Holy Land. With his son, Rudolf IV (later King Rudolf I), who has become famous in history, legend, and literature as "Rudolf of Habsburg," and who has rightly been regarded by all later Habsburgs as their real ancestor, because he established them as a power in Europe, a new chapter of Habsburg, and at the same time German, Austrian, and European, history begins.

4: *King Rudolf I, the Ancestor*

"He was tall, with long legs, delicately made, with a small head, a pale face, and a long nose; little hair, long, slim hands; a man temperate in food and drink and other things, a wise and intelligent man, . . ." thus a contemporary chronicler depicts the appearance and character of Rudolf of Habsburg. "He was valiant from his youth on, a man intelligent and powerful, but also favored by fortune, of tall stature, with a hooked nose, with a grave expression, whose dignity revealed the strength of his character"—so says another. The figure on the tomb in Speyer cathedral fully agrees with these descriptions. It shows a lean face, with finely chiseled, boldly curved nose, arched eyebrows, and a thin-lipped mouth drawn down at the corners. Recognizable are energy and single-mindedness, perhaps also a certain harshness, which seem entirely reconcilable with the inclination to kindly humor reported in so many stories and anecdotes. When the imperial graves in Speyer were opened in 1900, the findings confirmed contemporary reports of Rudolf's tall, slender, and fine-limbed figure.

As with his descendants Maximilian I and Joseph II, legend took hold of the figure of the Ancestor and drew the picture of an intelligent, kindhearted, popular, humorous, simple, pious, and humble knight. Harshness and singleness of purpose, the restless striving for increase of power and possessions, which doubtless also distinguished the historic Rudolf, were blurred and forgotten. Rudolf's alliance with the burghers of the rising cities in the southwest of the Empire, above all those of Zürich and Strassburg, kept his memory green after his death. Thus arose the image of the "pious

Count," which became a model for Habsburgs to emulate in their traditional style of piety; Schiller glorified it in his superb ballad "Der Graf von Habsburg" ("The Count of Habsburg"), and Grillparzer dramatized it in his play, *König Ottokars Glück und Ende* (*King Ottokar's Good Fortune and Death*). Heurteur, the Burgtheater actor who was the first to play Rudolf in *Ottokar*, earned Grillparzer's applause by replying to a question that he intended to perform the role as "half Emperor Francis and half St. Florian."

When Rudolf's picture, as drawn by popular tradition and distributed by Habsburg propaganda, is compared with the results of critical historical scholarship, it turns out—as always when legend transforms historic reality—that original traits have been intensified and coarsened by their later remodeling. The two pictures resemble each other as much as a popular copy of a famous painting—Leonardo's Last Supper or a Raphael Madonna—resembles its original. The shadings have been omitted, the plasticity of the figures has been lost, the dominant colors have been slapped on crudely and vigorously. Nevertheless the original is recognizable—the proverbial "true kernel" of almost all popular tradition.

Tradition particularly stresses two attributes of Rudolf's that were of decided political significance—his friendliness and his piety. There is a close connection between them. Both implicitly exalt Rudolf in comparison with the Emperors of the High Middle Ages, especially the Hohenstaufens, but also with his great antagonist Ottokar, King of Bohemia. Rudolf's own son, harsh King Albert, whose terrible end was felt to be not entirely undeserved, also served as a dark foil to the bright figure of his father.

Only a generation after Rudolf's death his affability, sense of humor, and quick wit were immortalized in a collection of humorous anecdotes. These reflect not only the political friendship of the burghers of Zürich and Strassburg but also the gratitude of the common people to the ruler who

had put an end to *"die Kaiserlose, die schreckliche Zeit"*
("the dreadful age without an emperor"). Alamannian soberness, restriction to the possible, the clever, circumspect
maintenance of one's own advantage—all made Rudolf appear to the burghers of his own and later times as the
ideal honest paterfamilias. The king who could advise a
Strassburg merchant on how to make a large profit in the
prevailing market (he was to supply Cologne with fish from
Strassburg and Strassburg with wine from Cologne, because
just then Strassburg had a glut of fish and a dearth of wine,
and Cologne a glut of wine and a dearth of fish) was even
believed capable of abandoning the expedition to Rome—
which he had in reality done so much to bring about—
because of his intelligent circumspection and caution.

The enemies of the Habsburgs, and all those who meas-
ured Rudolf's policies against the global plans of the Hohenstaufens, decried the image of the "shopkeeper-king."
Dante, the great, wrathful herald of imperial splendor, reproached Rudolf and Albert with having remained north of
the Alps only because of their greed and their desire for
territorial gain; by abandoning the expedition to Rome they
had helped to allow the "realm's garden" of Italy to go to
seed. This is the most famous version of the accusation.

The second motif in the image of Rudolf is his piety.
Two principal legends, handed down, recorded, and retold
in many different versions throughout the centuries, contributed essentially to strengthening the Habsburgs' religious consciousness of their mission. One is the famous tale
of Rudolf's encounter with the priest who was on his way
to administer the Last Sacrament. Rudolf offered him his
horse to cross a raging stream, and then gave him the
horse as a present because he did not wish to use for fighting or hunting a horse that had carried the Lord. The oldest
and simplest version of this tale was recorded about fifty
years after Rudolf's death. Later a causal connection with

his election to the throne was added, so that his elevation to the highest temporal office in Christendom became a reward for the reverence shown to the Holy of Holies; this version of the legend intensified the special veneration of the Habsburgs for the Blessed Sacrament. The legend is so obviously related to the contemporary establishment (by Pope Urban IV in 1264) of the Feast of Corpus Christi that when, during the Counter Reformation, this connection of the Habsburgs with the Blessed Sacrament assumed great programmatic significance, the legend was transferred to the year 1264 and various political speculations were attached to it. The renunciation of the war horse and hunter, consecrated to higher service, probably symbolized Rudolf's change, after his elevation to the sacred office of ruler, from the feud-happy, warlike dynast, to the herald and guardian of peace and law; here hunting, as is generally true in medieval myths and legends, symbolizes the related skill of war.

A similar motif recurs in the second famous tale. After Rudolf's election and coronation, and he was about to invest the peers of the realm, the scepter could not be found. Rudolf is supposed to have looked about him, taken a crucifix from the wall, kissed it, and said, "Here is the sign that has redeemed us and the whole world; let this be our scepter." That the first act of rule of the Habsburg dynasty took place under the sign of the cross was later interpreted symbolically and prophetically. Contemporaries, who saw Rudolf's elevation as an act of divine providence, reported that during his coronation a white cruciform cloud, shot with red by the morning sun, hovered over the cathedral in Aachen. This portent was first associated with Rudolf's plans for a crusade and an expedition to Rome, but later was also interpreted as signifying that the Habsburgs from the very beginning had ruled under the sign of the victorious cross, so that they were the legitimate successors and heirs of the first Christian Emperor, Constantine the

Great, and his device, *In hoc signo vinces*. (This motto recurs again and again in Baroque pictures of the Habsburg apotheosis, with an evident contemporary reference to the recent victory over the infidel Turks.)

These stories and ideas were based not only on the belief of his contemporaries that the conclusion of the interregnum and the election of the Habsburg Count, still little known outside Swabia, were acts of divine providence, but also on a definite historic fact: Rudolf's own words after his unexpected elevation. During his first days as Emperor he told the assembled crowd, "Today I intend to forgive every offense done to me by anyone who has harmed me. All prisoners who languish in my dungeons shall be freed; I vow from henceforth to be as much of a protector of the peace as I was until now an insatiable warrior"—words that echoed the general deep longing for peace and that therefore contributed decisively to the image of Rudolf formed in his own time and in later ages.

Rudolf's transformation, at the moment of his becoming Emperor, from "a true son of the feud-ridden period of the interregnum" (Oswald Redlich) to the bringer of peace, has been celebrated by Grillparzer in undyingly beautiful verses on the sublimity and religious dedication of the office of ruler; a classic formulation of the principle of the divine right of kings, written at a time when this theory was no longer self-evident, but rather—after the deep chasm of Enlightenment and Revolution—an archaism and a hope, a reminiscence and a challenge, all in one.

> *I am not he that once before you knew!*
> *No Habsburg, neither Rudolf am I now;*
> *Germany's blood alone flows in these veins.*
> *Germany's pulsebeat throbs within my heart.*
> *All that was mortal I have now put off,*
> *And am alone immortal Emperor.*

When the call summoned me to this great height,
When on my lowly head the Lord of the world
(Though I had never dreamed of such a gift)
Suddenly set his kingdom's diadem;
When the anointing oil dripped from my brow,
Then deeply did I feel the wonder's power
And learned to trust in wonders.

GRILLPARZER,
King Ottokar's Good Fortune and Death, Act III

"I am not he that once before you knew!" How far does this juxtaposition of Count and King, of "insatiable warrior" and bringer of peace, which was echoed in Rudolf's own words after his coronation and in the ideas of his contemporaries, coincide with historic reality? Does it do justice to the unity of the human personality, and especially to the gradual unfolding of Rudolf's political abilities, and his step-by-step exploration of and success in the European political scene? Probably here too, truth lies somewhere between the idealistic and the skeptical views.

Rudolf was twenty-two when he inherited from his father and was immediately plunged into the great conflicts of his time. True to his father's and grandfather's commitments, he allied himself with the Hohenstaufens, in spite of interdict and excommunication; he repeatedly visited his godfather Frederick II and later to Conrad IV when they were in Italy, and even accompanied young Conradin on his ill-starred campaign to Verona. (The tradition of Rudolf's participation in the fateful Battle of Tagliacozzo is probably false.) As Landgrave in Upper Alsace, and Count in Frickgau, Aargau, and the northern Zürich district, the Habsburg was in a position to grant safe-conduct from Strassburg to the Alps and was therefore an important figure. His conflict with his uncle (of the same name, the head of the Habsburg-Laufenburg branch), and Rudolf's own efforts to expand and round off his dominions, resulted in local contests on the Upper Rhine, which were closely connected with the great quarrel between the Hohenstaufens and the Papacy. But the expected large inheritance from the Counts of Kiburg promised more than compensation for the weakening of the Habsburg position caused by the division into two branches in 1232–39. In the struggle for the Kiburg possessions (in present-day western Switzerland), Rudolf opposed Count Peter of Savoy. This began the long series of fateful relations between the two houses which, like the relations with the Hohenzollerns, whether hostile or friendly, was to be significant in the history of both dynasties until Habsburg rule ended seven centuries later.

Besides safeguarding the Kiburg inheritance Rudolf also extended his dominions in numerous other feuds and conflicts with temporal and spiritual lords (as for instance with the two belligerent bishops, Walther von Geroldseck of Strassburg and Heinrich von Neuenburg of Basel). After the fall of the Hohenstaufens their former family or imperial estates were usually the prizes for such struggles. But Rudolf proved himself an intelligent political realist not only in acquiring but also in making better use of estates, through the introduction of tax and administrative organizations patterned after Frederick II's Sicilian model. The wealth thus gained was often used to purchase from rivals estates ruined through mismanagement and feuds.

Rudolf was fifty-five when he was elected king. During the conflict-ridden period from 1240 to 1273, the Count of Habsburg had acquired a political and military mastery that, as king, he brought to bear as successfully in European politics as in the decisive battle of the Marchfeld. While he was besieging the Bishop of Basel, Heinrich von Neuenburg, in one of the innumerable feuds carried through with all the severity and cruelty of the period, Rudolf received the news of his impending election to the throne. Since

Basel was totally surrounded and some of its burghers had been won over by Rudolf's bribery and promises, Bishop Heinrich's position in those September days of 1273 was highly precarious. At that point, about the twentieth of September, the Hohenzollern Burgrave Friedrich von Nürnberg arrived in the camp outside Basel as emissary of the Rhenish prince electors and (in the middle of the night, according to the story) offered the German royal crown to the Habsburg in his tent. Rudolf accepted the far from modest conditions of the electors and sent the Burgrave to the Bishop in Basel to negotiate a truce.

Astounded at this unexpected turn of events, Bishop Heinrich is supposed to have exclaimed, "Sit tight, Lord God in Heaven, or this Rudolf will usurp your place!" A truce was concluded and the cities that up to that moment had been feuding bitterly with Rudolf opened their gates to the chosen king.

For Habsburg territorial policies on the Upper Rhine, however, the royal election of 1273 meant an interruption whose effects were to be felt only much later. The estates in Upper Alsace, Breisgau, and the "upper lands" were not yet unified into a domain; the territory of the Bishop of Basel at the bend of the Rhine continued to separate the Alsatian from the Swiss possessions of the Habsburgs; even the success already achieved against the Bishop of Strassburg—whom Rudolf had prevented from conquering the imperial cities of Colmar, Mulhouse, and Kaiserberg—could no longer serve Habsburg territorial aggrandizement after Rudolf's election. The three Alsatian cities in the middle of the Habsburg lands remained directly subject to the Empire and blocked complete unification of the territory. Furthermore, Rudolf's promise to his electors, the Rhenish princes, that he would leave them in possession of the imperial and Hohenstaufen property they had appropriated during the interregnum, set up an insurmountable barrier to his own drive for expansion in southwestern Germany.

Since he intended to establish his kingdom on a firm foundation of power, the only possible compensation left was in the eastern part of the realm, where in the war with Ottokar the interests of the Empire and the Habsburg efforts to acquire a unified domain could be combined. The shift in emphasis from west to east—a dominant motif in Habsburg history during later centuries (as also in that of the Luxemburg and Wittelsbach dynasties, then competing with the Habsburgs)—was already inherent in the situation when the royal election took place in 1273.

Did elevation to the highest temporal office in Christendom really change Rudolf? One ought not to underestimate the sacred significance of royalty for contemporary consciousness and thus for Rudolf himself. On the other hand, the greater circumspection and caution that Rudolf displayed as king may be sufficiently explained by the maturity of advancing years and the consideration that the game was now for much higher stakes. Even as king, Rudolf remained able to make bold decisions, as he demonstrated in his conflict with Ottokar. On the other hand, while still a count, he avoided using force where money and fair words might achieve his object, and, when the multitude of petty feuds threatened to lame his energies, he made a quick peace to free his hands for the conflict with the most important opponent. But his reversion to a policy of acquiring and expanding Habsburg estates in the southwest, taken up again with passionate violence in the last years of his life, shows that as king he remained true to the objectives that he had set himself as a young count.

The effort to free himself from other threats in order to concentrate on the decisive conflict with the most dangerous enemy, a basic maxim of all successful politics, governed Rudolf's conduct during the first years when he was securing his kingship. He had been elected because the German princes wished to reconstruct a generally recognized royal power, strong enough to legitimize their possessions acquired during the interregnum, but not strong enough to endanger them, and because Pope Gregory X decidedly wished to re-establish order in Germany. If Rudolf's monarchy were to last, therefore, he had above all to secure the support of the princes, especially the prince electors, and the Papacy.

In addition to keeping his election promises to leave the prince electors in possession of the estates acquired during the interregnum, and to make the very generously interpreted repayment for the costs of the election, Rudolf bound the prince electors of the Palatinate, Saxony, and Brandenburg to him by marriage, thus making good use of the capital his six daughters constituted. He won over the Pope through promises of a crusade and an expedition to Rome, as well as through making it clear from the beginning that he did not intend to resume the traditional Italian policy of the Hohenstaufens. Rudolf did not by any means neglect Italy as much as has often been alleged (Dante's criticism has already been mentioned), and in fact he tried to reconstitute imperial privileges unobtrusively and by degrees, particularly in northern Italy. But his renunciation of the Hohenstaufen Italian policy and his attempt to come to terms with the Papacy nevertheless contributed decisively to fix the images both of "pious King Rudolf" and of the *Verzichtpolitiker*[1] who liquidated the high medieval dreams of Empire. Certainly the fall of the Hohenstaufens, which he himself had lived and suffered through as a Hohenstaufen partisan, must have been an ever-present warning.

[1] A politician who abandons a position rather than risk a struggle.

After the Pope had clearly decided in favor of Rudolf at the Council of Lyon in the early summer of 1274 (one of his champions on that occasion having been the great German philosopher and naturalist Albertus Magnus[2]), the king had his hands free for the unavoidable contest with the king of Bohemia, the Premyslid Ottokar II. Like the Count of Habsburg in the narrower conditions of the west, splintered into factions by power politics, the Bohemian king had used the opportunity provided by the interregnum and the more extensive spaces of eastern Europe, with its larger, more compact domains, to extend his own sovereignty. He had been benefited both by the fall of the Hohenstaufens and the extinction of the ducal family of Babenberg in Austria. Thus an Empire was developing which threatened to endanger the German princes and the German monarchy between the Baltic and the Adriatic. Since Rudolf's election had vitiated Ottokar's hopes of gaining the German royal crown himself, a battle between the two— to which the newly elected king was also obligated by the stipulations of imperial law—was inevitable.

The careful diplomatic and military preparations and the way in which Ottokar, in spite of his incomparably greater financial means, was outmaneuvered even before an important battle occurred, demonstrated Rudolf's organizational, political, and military mastery on the level of world politics. As in the petty feuds in his ancestral lands, the Habsburg was victorious principally because of his sober and accurate judgment of his own and the enemy's dispositions of strength, because of his proven, dependable allies (Ludwig, Count of the Palatinate, Count Meinhard of Tyrol, and the Burgrave Friedrich von Nürnberg) and because he won over the enemy's allies, Duke Heinrich of Lower Bavaria, the Austrian and Styrian nobility, and even the

[2] Albert von Bollstädt.

Bohemian nobles, particularly the Rosenberg family in southern Bohemia.

So superior a leader was Rudolf, proceeding move by move like a chess champion, that a rare and ideal event in the history of warfare occurred when the enemy was defeated without risking a final decision on the field of battle. Ottokar gave up Austria, Styria, Carinthia, Carniola, the Wendish March, Eger, and Pordenone, and was invested by the king with Bohemia, Moravia, and the imperial fiefs appertaining to these two territories. A double marriage—a daughter of Ottokar to one of Rudolf's sons, a daughter of Rudolf's to one of Ottokar's sons—was supposed to strengthen the peace. However, Rudolf's wise moderation in the peace treaty, after the fortunate outcome of the campaign of 1276, could not prevent the resumption of war, for a number of reasons—probably the most important being the imperial princes' concern at Rudolf's increased power. In any case, his position had deteriorated considerably when a new outbreak of hostilities threatened in the first half of 1278. But again Rudolf proved his political and military superiority. To compensate for the lack of the imperial armies he mobilized his Hungarian allies, King Ladislas and the Hungarian Magnates; he rapidly brought up reinforcements to secure Vienna, where the presence of numerous secret partisans of Ottokar had made his position unsafe; and finally, while Ottokar lost valuable time besieging Drosendorf and Laa in northern Lower Austria, Rudolf advanced to Marchegg to meet the Hungarians and secured for them the crossing over the March. In the ensuing great battle at Dürnkrut and Jedenspeigen on the Marchfeld, during which Ottokar lost his life, Rudolf made certain of his victory by forming a reserve—unusual tactics in those times—that was thrown in only at the height of battle to make a flank attack on the enemy.

Although Ottokar's army contained not only Poles and

Silesians but also German allies of the Bohemian king (from Brandenburg, Meissen, Thuringia, and Bavaria), and although on Rudolf's side the Hungarian and Cuman allies contributed importantly to the victory, the battle of the Marchfeld was properly evaluated by contemporaries and later ages alike as a victory of the Empire over it insubordinate Bohemian vassal. Only centuries later was the Prussian-Austrian antagonism reflected backward to the fight between the Habsburg and the Premyslid, and an attempt made to see the Bohemian king as a prototype of the ideals that lay behind the formation of the Little-German (*klein-deutsch*) and Prussian monarchies.

But the day of the battle of the Marchfeld, the twenty-sixth of August, 1278, became the real birthday of Habsburg rule in Austria, the birthday of the dynasty that finally took over the name of the country and that, as "*Haus Oesterreich*," "*Casa d'Austria*," and "*Maison d'Autriche*," carried the name of the little country on the Danube around the whole globe. On the Marchfeld, where the Alps, the Sudetenland, and the Carpathians join like the three parts of a cloverleaf, all the different peoples of these areas were embattled: Germans of all tribes, Czechs, Moravians, Poles, Hungarians, and Cumans. In Ottokar's army the battle cry was "*Praga, Praga*," while "*Rom, Rom*" and "*Christus, Christus*" were shouted by the German king's soldiers. When on Rudolf's side the warlike Bishop of Basel struck up the battle hymn, "*Sant Maria, Mutter und Magd, all unsre Not sei Dir geklagt*" (Holy Mary, Mother and Maid, may all our grief be poured out to you), the Bohemians answered with their hymn, "*Hospodine pomiluy ny*" (Lord, have mercy on us).

From the Moravian city of Feldsberg King Rudolf sent reports of his victory not only to Pope Nicholas III and to Archbishop Friedrich of Salzburg, but also to the Doge of Venice and the city of Florence, and since Rudolf's victory was regarded as a prerequisite of the anticipated expedition to Rome and the imperial coronation, Italian chroniclers reported on it extensively.

In securing the newly acquired territories for his House, King Rudolf again proceeded with his customary wisdom and circumspection. His old brother-in-arms, Count Meinhard of Görz-Tyrol, was demanding recompense for the help he had supplied, and the problem lay in the difficulty of partly satisfying and partly rejecting his claims. Rudolf gained the support of the political powers in the different countries by generously confirming the privileges of the temporal and spiritual lords and of the cities, and by revoking Ottokar's measures for strengthening the position of the sovereign.

After conquering Ottokar and settling affairs in Bohemia and Moravia (in accordance with the double marriage previously arranged) Rudolf remained in Vienna for the next few years. From there he also visited Styria and prepared to transfer its rich and important lands to his House, while at the same time continuing his plans for the larger theater of European politics: the marriage of his son Hartmann to the English princess Joanna, and that of his youngest daughter, Clementia, to the grandson of Charles of Anjou, Charles III, "Martell."

During his five years in Austria fate struck heavily at the family of the septuagenarian king; two sons died in infancy and then, shortly after Clementia left for Naples, his wife Anna died. She had given her husband eleven children. Just before Christmas of that same year, 1281 (after Rudolf had at long last returned to the western part of his Empire in June, and had left his eldest son, Albert, as imperial regent in Austria and Styria), his second son Hartmann, aged eighteen, who had been betrothed to the English princess Joanna, was drowned in the icy waves of the Rhine when his boat overturned. He was just returning from border fights against the Count of Savoy and was crossing from Breisach to Oppenheim to join his father.

A year later all the obstacles to the investiture of the king's sons with Austrian lands had finally been overcome, and a few days before Christmas 1282, in Augsburg, the Counts Albert and Rudolf of Habsburg received Austria, Styria, Carniola and the Wendish March—also, as a matter of form, Carinthia, which the sons however resigned in favor of Meinhard of Tyrol. It was a joint investiture. When the Austrian lords protested against it, Rudolf determined, in the domestic edict of Rheinfelden (on June 1, 1283), that Albert was to rule in the Austrian lands and that Rudolf the younger was to be recompensed elsewhere. But Albert's male heirs were again to receive the Austrian lands in joint investiture. There was an obvious endeavor to avoid division of inheritance—probably because the king still remembered the disadvantages of the separation of the family branches in 1232–39. However, this compromise between the wishes of the Austrian lords and the Habsburg domestic edict led finally—through the discrimination against the younger Rudolf—to a disastrous event for Habsburg and German history, the murder of Albert by his brother Rudolf's son, young John (the Parricide).

King Rudolf dedicated the last years of his life chiefly to efforts to safeguard his son Albert's succession in the Empire, which was not achieved because Albert could be elected during his father's lifetime only after his father's imperial coronation in Rome. Further, he tried to round off and extend the Habsburg family possessions in the southwest of the realm. These enterprises (like the frequent attempts to acquire Bohemia and Hungary) were intended to strengthen royal power at the expense of the prince electors, and thus to secure Habsburg succession to the throne. So Rudolf returned at last, this time as king, to his early policy of augmenting the ancestral Habsburg lands.

Through purchase as well as through enforcing all claims that were his by virtue of his royal office or laws of inheritance, he made still further gains, especially in the territory of present-day Switzerland. To be sure, in his last years this almost feverish policy of acquisition and expansion stimulated the resistance and alliance of his enemies, in the "upper lands" as well as in the Empire. After Rudolf's death both the rise of the Swiss Confederacy and the election of Adolf of Nassau to the German throne proved the strength of the opposition forces that had been convoked as a reaction to Habsburg success.

After successfully maintaining the imperial rights in the west against France and Burgundy, Rudolf also appeared in the last year of his life as a herald and protector of peace in northern Germany. His ride to Speyer when he felt a premonition of approaching death ("*Wohlauf nach Speyer, wo mehrere meiner Vorfahren sind, die auch Könige waren*"— (Godspeed to Speyer, where lie several of my ancestors, who were also kings) shows once again his conviction of the greatness and importance of his House and of the majesty of the royal office.

"I am my family's Rudolf of Habsburg," the Corsican upstart, Napoleon, once said, though he himself, by marrying a Habsburg, tried to achieve "equality of birth" with the ruling dynasties of Europe. The comparison is doubly lame. Not only had Rudolf's ancestors been powerful lords on the Upper Rhine for three centuries, but Rudolf himself, in the half-century of his political activity, aggrandizement and rule, proved himself always—in small things as in big, not withstanding the daring of individual decisions— a sober realist in politics, and a master in "the art of the possible," which is, according to Bismarck's apt definition, the essence of politics.

5: *Failure and Renunciation*

Though King Rudolf successfully increased the possessions of his House and raised it to new heights, he was unable to achieve his final political goal, his own coronation as Emperor and—in spite of the strenuous attempts in the last years of his life—the safeguarding of his son's succession. Certainly he left an important and rich inheritance to Albert. Habsburg jurisdiction in the west had been greatly expanded; in the east a large complex of lands, the dukedoms of Austria and Styria (formally also Carniola, mortgaged to Carinthia) had been added to the House, and the acquisition of Bohemia and Hungary seemed as possible as the connection of western and eastern domains by means of a land bridge of estates. For Albert's wife was a daughter of Meinhard of Tyrol, and, in the course of the fourteenth century, the Habsburgs acquired first Carinthia and then the Tyrol, adding both areas permanently to their holdings. However, control over Bohemia, obtained in Albert's days when the Premyslid line died out, lasted only a short time, and the hope of acquiring Hungary could not as yet be realized.

In addition to a throne, claims, and expectations, Rudolf left his son an invaluable bequest, a gift for politics. Probably it resulted from a happy union between heredity and education. Albert, when his father was elected king, had just reached a decisive point in the formation of character—the threshold between youth and manhood. As his father's collaborator, assistant, and political pupil, he shared in the House of Habsburg's entry into major European politics, in the development of a system of alliances, antagonisms, and relationships reaching from England to Sicily and from Provence to Hungary, in which a quarrel with the abbot of St. Gall found a place as well as the *modus vivendi* with the Pope in Rome, the great conflict with Ottokar, and the acquisition and maintenance of the Austrian lands.

Nearly all the qualities that made up Rudolf's political genius are to be found again, almost intensified, in Albert: wise deliberation; accurate weighing of possible courses of action, combined with strength of will and resolution; unscrupulous harshness—but also intelligent moderation, whenever circumstances demanded it; the ability to wait and let the situation mature, but to seize the initiative energetically at the decisive moment. Albert seems to have lacked only one very important quality of Rudolf's—the warmth and friendliness, combined with a sense of humor, with which Rudolf had won men's hearts. Albert's image, unlike his father's, was not adorned with a garland of popular legends and anecdotes. Though politically perhaps the most important of the earlier Habsburgs, for the authors of popular and didactic books in later centuries he constituted a real dilemma quite apart from his frightful death. While the German princes, like the Bohemian King Ottokar, might at first have underestimated Rudolf and have thought him a tractable tool or a not particularly dangerous enemy, such self-deception was impossible with Albert, partly because the Habsburgs had gained so much power in the interim, but also because of his personality. Friend and foe alike had to recognize from the beginning that they were dealing with a man who, fully convinced of his legitimate claim to the highest temporal office, strove resolutely and singlemindedly to consolidate and extend his power and to found a strong German kingdom under his dynasty.

According to reports, Albert was not prepossessing to look at. When he lost an eye in 1295 after inexpert medical

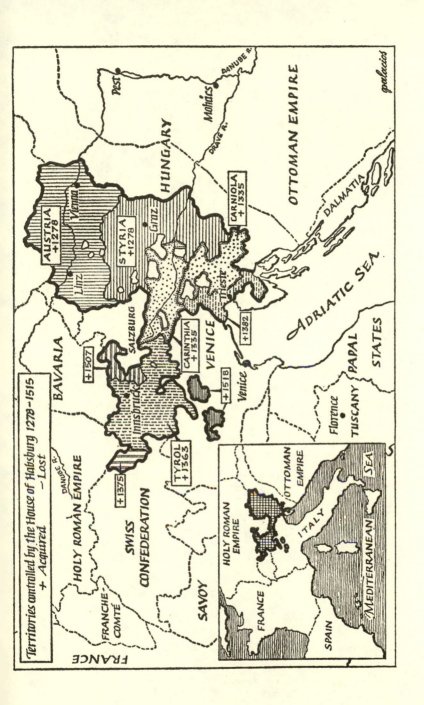

treatment, (to drain off the poison supposed to have caused his disease, the doctors had him hung by his feet, until he fainted; the congestion of blood destroyed one eye) he looked repellent and even alarming. The strong aversion of his brother-in-law, the Bohemian King Wenceslas (which introduced a personal element into the reviving political antagonism between Habsburgs and Premyslids) decisively delayed Albert's progress to the throne, and the aversion he engendered in his immediate circle and among his vassals eventually caused his doom.

Personal motives were thus closely intermixed in the general political situation that Albert inherited from Rudolf. All his life Albert had to steer the Habsburg ship of state, the ship of his political plans and aspirations, against the hostile winds that blew up on all sides in reaction to Rudolf's sudden good fortune. This was as true for Habsburg claims to the kingdom as for the management of their ancestral lands in the southwest and their newly acquired territories in the southeast, Austria and Styria.

On the Upper Rhine and in the Swiss territory King Rudolf's policy of acquisition, carried out very rigorously in the last years of his life, provoked strong resistance. On August 1, 1291, only seventeen days after Rudolf's death and immediately after news of it arrived, the three forest cantons of Uri, Schwyz, and Unterwalden formed their Eternal League and created the first Switzerland. (August first, today regarded as the official birthday of Switzerland, is celebrated as the great Swiss national holiday.) Perhaps at that moment the League was not directed expressly against the Habsburgs, but attempted chiefly to safeguard its newly gained freedom by mutual assistance in the troubled times that were expected. But during two centuries of protracted struggle, this germ of a political development led to a decisive weakening of the Habsburg position in the heart of Europe. In October of that same year an offensive and defensive alliance was concluded by Uri and Schwyz with Zürich and the traditional Habsburg enemies in the "upper lands," Savoy, St. Gall, and others. It was clearly aimed against Albert, whose involvement in these wars weakened his position in the struggle now beginning for the imperial succession.

Both in the ancestral lands and in the Empire Rudolf's death became the signal for an alliance of all those forces that judged that the Habsburg kingdom had already become too strong under Rudolf. As the prince electors had once turned against the mighty Bohemian King Ottokar, so now they rejected the "Austrian" Albert, ruler over an extensive and powerful eastern domain, who appeared hardly less dangerous to them and their position. As they had put up against the Bohemian king the Habsburg count from the Upper Rhine, so now they elected the even less powerful Rhenish count, Adolf of Nassau.

Adolf's kingship, which ended, according to an almost inevitable law of politics, in conflict with the prince electors after his effort to achieve hegemony in the east (by annexing Meissen and Thuringia), has been called a mere loss of time and an "interference with the early objectives attained by Rudolf." This is true if one measures the growth of a strong German kingdom by the standards of development in the English or French monarchies, and sees only promises that were not destined to be fulfilled. But from the Habsburg point of view, the Nassau kingdom provided a not unimportant breathing space, enabling Albert to consolidate his rule in southwest and southeast alike, though he had to carry it through with an eye on the still inevitable conflict with Adolf and on the chief purpose of recapturing the crown for the House of Habsburg. In tolerating the Count of Nassau's election, whose validity Albert probably never acknowledged to himself, in surrendering the royal insignia to him, in strengthening the Habsburg position during the following years in his own domains, and in preparing diplomatically for the conflict with Adolf, Albert proved himself the true son and heir of Rudolf, the political realist.

Though in the west Albert was regarded as the powerful Duke of Austria and Styria, to be dreaded and kept at a distance through the protection afforded by alliances, in Austria and Styria themselves he was looked upon by the nobility and the sovereign cities as the "foreigner," the "Swabian," who had brought with him vassals from his Rhenish lands to uphold his rule, and who surrounded himself with these "foreigners." The major crisis for a ruling dynasty usually breaks out in the second generation; then the people's hopes aroused by the change of rulers prove illusory, and the cautious efforts of the first new ruler to gain the affection of his subjects change to an attempt at more rigorous exertion of his sovereign rights. At the same time, the new dynasty is not yet regarded as completely "native" and "hereditary." To gain the support of the Austrians and Styrians against Ottokar, Rudolf had made far-reaching concessions to them. Now Albert had to rescind these concessions as far as possible and exert his ducal rights more forcefully.

In the conflicts resulting in both Austria and Styria during the first fifteen years of Habsburg rule, Albert conclusively demonstrated his remarkable military and political gifts. In quelling the Viennese rebellion (1287), the Styrian uprising (1292), and the rising of the Austrian nobility (1295–96), as well as in the feud with the Archbishop of Salzburg (1288–89), Albert defeated his enemies by his great speed and mobility, particularly in the two surprise victories that he gained by unexpected winter crossings of the Pyhrn and Semmering passes. But quick, energetic, and drastic measures were always supplemented by wise moderation and generous concessions to the defeated rebels, so that Albert succeeded in preventing once-defeated enemies from taking part in a later revolt. How clearly he saw the need to make his House "native" to Austria is shown by the single fact that in christening his sons he used, in addition to the old Habsburg names of Rudolf, Albrecht, and Otto, the traditional Babenberg names of Friedrich, Leopold, and Heinrich.

From the base of his well-established rule in Austria and Styria, with his alliance to the Hungarian King Andrew III (married to one of his daughters) protecting his rear, Albert renewed his attack against Adolf, whose deteriorating relations with the prince electors he utilized as skillfully as he did the great conflict between England and France. These intelligent and energetically pursued policies were rewarded by the prince electors' deposition of Adolf, the cavalry Battle of Göllheim, in which Adolf lost both crown and life, and finally by Albert's own election to the throne.

As king, Albert displayed the same energy, especially in breaking the power of the prince electors—an indispensable prerequisite for the establishment of a strong monarchy in Germany. Here also he received invaluable protection from his alliance with the French King Philip IV (reinforced by the marriage of Albert's son Rudolf to the French Princess Blanche). Although the early death of Rudolf, for whom he had secured the Bohemian succession after the Premyslid line became extinct, once more vitiated the hope of permanently acquiring Bohemia, Albert would undoubtedly have been the right man to achieve it for his House, despite all obstacles, and to obtain Meissen and Thuringia (following the Nassau policy). If we also recall that a few years before Albert had tried, though vainly, to acquire the vacant imperial fief of Holland for his House, then his grand conception becomes clear: encirclement of the kingdom by strong Habsburg forces in the northwest and northeast, as had already been accomplished in the southwest and southeast; political neutralization of the prince electors, and thereby the creation of a strong German and Habsburg monarchy. Albert's attitude to the great contemporary struggle between the French king and Pope Boniface VIII, and his changeover from the French to the papal side, was conditioned by his plans to complete what Rudolf had left unachieved. Since Albert at that time was just the same age as his father had been on entering the stage of European politics, any student of the period will wonder if Albert, had he remained alive, could have given a different direction to German and European history by establishing a strong monarchy.

Therefore May 1, 1308, has well been called (by Hans Hirsch) a black day in German history, for on that date King Albert, after crossing the Reuss to the high plain of Windisch, in sight of the Habsburg castle, died under the daggers of his nephew John and three fellow conspirators, noblemen from the "upper lands." In this murder by John, who had barely come of age and who believed that Albert had cheated him of part of his inheritance, the tension between the legal rights of the family as a whole and the political necessity of gathering all power in one strong hand found catastrophic expression. Undoubtedly John's unhappy decision was encouraged by the strong opposition that Albert's energetic policies evoked on all sides, especially in the home of John's fellow conspirators.

For the Habsburg family the Windisch murder was a turning point, the first great setback in a series of events that concluded the first Habsburg monarchy. At the same time Habsburg power in southwestern Germany began to decline, and both developments indirectly assisted the Habsburg accumulation of land in the southeast, on which the family was now forced to concentrate its strength.

The prince electors, suddenly freed by Albert's murder from a mortal danger to their own power, very understandably now elected not a Habsburg but a less powerful western count, Henry of Luxemburg. Since he succeeded in obtaining Bohemia for his House, Habsburg policy in the east was partly determined by a love-hate relationship with the Luxemburgers in Bohemia, which lasted for more than a century. In the west Henry, like Adolf of Nassau before him, encouraged the enemies of the Habsburgs, especially in the Swiss Confederation, now rapidly growing in strength. The terrible vengeance taken by Albert's children on the families of the regicides doubtless helped to intensify anti-Habsburg sentiments in the "upper lands," where, according to the prevailing legal interpretation, what the Habsburgs saw as murder was regarded only as manslaughter. Seven years after the Windisch murder the "upper lands" became the scene of a new heavy blow to the prestige of the Habsburgs in their own ancestral territory—the first defeat of their knights by Confederate troops in the Battle of Morgarten (1315).

In turn, the defeat of Morgarten was closely related to the attempt that the Habsburg third generation (after Rudolf and Albert) had made shortly before to gain the crown for Albert's son Frederick the Handsome, apparently possible after Henry VII's early death in Italy. But this time the undertaking failed. Because the Luxemburgers could not hope to push through the election of Henry's eighteen-year-old son John, particularly since (as king of Bohemia) he might become dangerous to the power of the prince electors, they supported the candidacy of a Wittelsbach, Louis of Bavaria, who had already crossed swords with his Austrian cousin Frederick (they were both grandsons of Rudolf of Habsburg, since Louis's mother Mechthild had been one of Rudolf's six daughters). The Wittelsbachs, whose land was surrounded in both the west and the east by Habsburg domains, were natural rivals of the Habsburgs.

After the double election of 1314 the fight between Louis and Frederick dragged on for eight years. Finally, on September 28, 1322, near Mühldorf on the Inn in Bavaria, there was a decisive battle in which Louis defeated and captured his rival. After three years of captivity in Castle Trausnitz in the Upper Palatinate, Frederick—whose brothers Leopold and Albert were continuing the fight against the Wittelsbachs—was ready to sign a treaty in which he renounced his royal honors and acknowledged the election of Louis, who in return confirmed his imperial fiefs. It was not easy for Frederick to bring his brothers (especially the warlike Leopold) to accept this renunciation of the crown by the House of Habsburg, and King Louis even agreed temporarily to concede to Frederick a formal right of imperial joint rule and the use of the royal title. Only after Leopold died in 1326, when barely thirty years old, and a quarrel among the surviving brothers had further weakened the Habsburg position, were the Habsburgs and King Louis completely reconciled; in the same year Frederick died in his castle Gutenstein, in Lower Austria, and was buried in the Carthusian monastery that he had founded in the Vienna woods.

The full weight of Frederick's renunciation of imperial sovereignty was felt so acutely by his contemporaries and by posterity that tradition compensated for it by stressing his chivalric loyalty to Louis. When Frederick could not gain his brothers' consent, he is said to have returned voluntarily to his prison, in spite of all entreaties, thereby keeping his word to Louis who, touched by so much loyalty, gave him the co-regency, treated him as a brother, and even shared bed and board with him. Though this story was partly supported by external events, it naturally did not take into account King Louis's difficult position, which prompted the reconciliation with his prisoner. But for Habsburg tradition the tale of the ruler who loyally kept his sworn word (even though the Pope released him from the promise made in captivity) and voluntarily returned to his enemy's prison, had its own political value. For the relationship between ruler and subject, between feudal lord and vassal, rests precisely on the principle of mutual faith and mutual trust.

The three dates 1308, 1315, and 1322—Albert's assassination, and the defeats of Morgarten and Mühldorf—mark the completion of the shift in emphasis from west to east that had already begun under Rudolf. The gradual loss of position in the west as well as the temporary abandonment of the attempt to obtain the German crown—two lines of development forced upon Habsburg evolution by the anti-Habsburg powers and often closely interrelated—now compelled the dynasty even more strongly to expand and round off its southeastern position. Albert's sons (who first received "Austrian," i.e., Babenberg, names) were the first to take true root in Austria. Certainly the southwestern positions were not given up or simply surrendered without a fight; nor did the Habsburgs relinquish in principle their attempt to acquire German sovereignty. They maintained the footholds from which, under favorable auguries, the offensive could once again be launched to achieve their ultimate aims, and the imperial titles and claims remaining from the period of Rudolf and Albert were neither dropped nor forgotten. The Habsburgs remained potentially royal. But the center of gravity for all their political efforts and ambitions had now definitely shifted to Austria and Styria, to the dukedoms of the southeast. This is clear from Habsburg family documents. While earlier wills named churches and monasteries, or religious foundations generally, in the ancestral lands and in the west of the kingdom as recipients of endowments for requiem masses, after this turn of events churches and monasteries in Austria and Styria were mentioned more and more frequently. Only at this point did the Habsburgs become large-scale founders, supporters, and patrons of Austrian churches and monastic establishments; only then did the memory of the family's "Swabian" origin fade and the Dukes of Austria become Austrians by their own conviction as well as in that of their subjects. Only then were conditions created for the later fusion of the concepts of the "House of Habsburg" and the "House of Austria," the names of dynasty and country, which became so complete that the "House of Austria" at times means not merely the dynasty but also the *Herrschaft*, the sum total of the whole complex of lands subject to Habsburg sovereignty.

Nevertheless, the family remained established in the west for some time to come, and it is there that we meet first with a remarkable woman champion and guardian of the Habsburg tradition of government, Albert I's energetic daughter Agnes. As the widowed Queen of Hungary she persecuted the regicides with merciless severity, and on the scene of the bloody deed of Windisch she founded, in atonement and commemoration, the monastery of Königsfelden, where she spent the rest of her life. As the real head of the family in the west, she also became the advisor to the following generation, and especially to her nephew Rudolf IV, "the Founder," in whose lofty plans her influence is certainly detectable.

6: *The "Arch-house" and Its Mythology*

Duke Albert II, "the Wise" (also called "the Lame," because he had been crippled in 1330, the year of his accession, as a result of some unknown disease—possibly brought on by poison), drew the proper conclusions from the defeat and abdication of his brother. He was ten years younger than Frederick the Handsome, and, as the fourth of King Albert's sons, had at first been destined for the Church; perhaps because of this upbringing and education, and certainly because of his physical handicap, he was not inclined to be a warrior. Moreover, the battles for the crown and the feud that had recently developed from the rebellion of the youngest brother, Duke Otto, "the Merry," against Frederick and Albert (in which the Hungarian as well as the Bohemian king had intervened), had ravaged the country and had once again demonstrated the dangers inherent in Austria's geographical position.

Thus Albert II became the first "prince of peace" among the Habsburgs, loved by his subjects (according to numerous anecdotes), and admired as a praiseworthy exception among the bellicose rulers of this period of feuds. Through the astute gambit of an alliance with the Luxemburg King John of Bohemia, at the very beginning of his rule, he concluded a lasting peace with the German King Louis in the Treaty of Hagenau (August 6, 1330). Albert's policy, intelligent and restrained, yet not lacking in firmness, and at first (when necessary) backed by his brother Otto's constant readiness to make war, led a few years later (1335) to the acquisition, of Carinthia and Carniola. Habsburg jurisdiction now extended from the Bohemian and Mo-

ravian borders to the Adriatic. At the same time he prepared to annex the Tyrol, an action later completed by his
son Rudolf. In the now openly erupting conflicts between
Luxemburgers and Wittelsbachs, Albert—even more averse
to open warfare after his brother Otto's death in 1339—
acted as mediator, which enabled him to keep himself and
his country out of war and at the same time to reap the
advantages of contact with both sides. He devoted the
greater part of his considerable political energies to strengthening his ducal control over internal affairs, to pursuing a
single-minded economic policy for the enrichment of his
household finances, to increasing the crown lands, and to
helping the ducal cities by granting charters to guilds and
granting or extending city privileges. Here are visible the
beginnings of a planned economic and social policy, within
the restricted framework of the medieval legal and social
order. Later they were so far developed by Albert's son,
Rudolf IV, that a modern sociologist and politician (Ernst
Karl Winter) could see in Rudolf IV the representative of
"Early Austrian socialism" and the ideal of the "ruler with
a social conscience." Eighteenth-century economic and
financial policies in the great epoch of reform under Maria
Theresa invoked the authority of Albert II's regulations for
commerce, showing a recognizable line of development in
economic and social policy which, always adapted to the
realities of the age, can be called a constant element in
Habsburg history.

Though Albert II continued his grandfather Rudolf's
realistic policy of limiting himself to what was possible, he
was not merely intent on increasing his House's power in
the east while neglecting the ancestral lands. Through his
marriage to Johanna, daughter and heiress of the Count of
Pfirt, he acquired a new county adjoining the Habsburg
lands in Upper Alsace, and also, before starting to rule in
Austria, he had administered the ancestral territory on the

Upper Rhine, as his brother Leopold's successor. Albert strove to maintain good relations with the Luxemburg Emperor Charles IV (already improved by the betrothal and marriage in childhood of Albert's son Rudolf to Charles's daughter Catherine) because only thus could he hope at last to end the patronage of the Swiss Confederacy by non-Habsburg (and therefore usually anti-Habsburg) kings, Adolf of Nassau, Henry VII, and Louis the Bavarian. In spite of his physical handicaps, which were aggravated by military campaigns, the Lame Duke with his young son Rudolf twice entered the "upper lands" with an army, though no major battles ensued. Arbitration by Charles IV on July 13, 1355, protected the Habsburg possessions in Switzerland from further losses for the time being.

On November 25 in that same year Albert issued a domestic edict in which, according to the traditional laws of the House, his four sons Rudolf, Frederick, Albert, and Leopold were to "remain united in brotherly love," and

> the eldest [should] be the same as the youngest, and the youngest the same as the eldest, that they should live with each other cordially, virtuously, and fraternally in all things and have in nothing any dispute, quarrel, or enmity, and that each one should respect the other as his equal in honor and dignity.

The territorial nobility were appointed guarantors for this domestic edict, and had to swear that they would never support one of the brothers against another.

In taking this measure Albert was probably guided as much by the memory of his father's terrible end as by his more recent experience of the disputes in which he himself had to fight at his brother Frederick's side against the rebellious youngest brother, Otto. The harmful effects on other princely Houses of the partitioning of property through inheritance surely did not escape the wise prince's notice; however, the idea of primogeniture, which was the only effective safeguard against the dangers of division, was still remote from the thought of the period and the Habsburg family tradition.

Signs of the principle of primogeniture appear only with Albert's eldest son, Rudolf IV, "the Founder."[1] This Rudolf is undoubtedly the most fascinating, and perhaps the most brilliant, among the many important early Habsburgs. In the seven years of his rule, which began in 1358 when he was nineteen, he achieved much in many different spheres, but, even more important, he developed plans and ideas that were taken up and realized only in later periods. In many respects much in advance of his time, precociously accomplished and then prematurely dead, he became the real founder of the "mythology" of his House.

At the very beginning of his reign, Rudolf undertook three measures that, though apparently unrelated, were in fact expressions of the same lofty design; the great forgeries of the Austrian letters of independence in the winter of 1358–59; the *Ungeld*-order of March 21, 1359[2]; and finally the rebuilding of St. Stephen's Cathedral, for which Rudolf himself, on March 11, 1359, turned the first spade of earth. This earned him his sobriquet, *fundator*, "the Founder."

Unwilling to accept the omission of his family from the college of prince electors, when Emperor Charles IV established it in his Golden Bull, Rudolf tried to use forged privileges, claims to the titles of "Duke of the Palatinate," "Duke of Swabia," and "Grand Master of the Hunt," as well as the claim to wear an arched crown and other insignia of sovereignty, to obtain for himself and for his House

---

[1] Habsburg domestic law and the principle of collective inheritance are also reflected in the numbering of Rudolf I's early deceased son as Rudolf II, and King Albert's oldest son (the King of Bohemia, who also died young) as Rudolf III, since both were invested with the duchy of Austria, though neither ever ruled there.

[2] A new tax on drinks in the crown lands, ducal cities, and church lands was introduced in exchange for the ruler's renunciation of the heretofore annual reissue (debasement) of coinage.

a special position with privileges exceeding even those of the prince electors. Though he wished to see the Austrian ruler protected from any interference by imperial power, his own right to dispose freely of crown land and also his authority over the landed nobility were to be increased in every way, and the ruler and his country were to take special rank as "the heart and shield of the Empire."

The reform of the tax structure, the attempt to curtail the nobility's influence over the cities, the reorganization of the guilds, as well as the foundation of a university in Vienna (on the model of that established in Prague by his imperial father-in-law and political opponent Charles IV, whom Rudolf tried to equal or outstrip in every way), the renovation of St. Stephen's Cathedral, and the establishment of a Viennese bishopric—all were parts of a comprehensive plan whose final aim, as Charles IV and other contemporaries clearly recognized, was the recapture of the German crown for the House of Habsburg.

Territorial acquisitions and enterprises also played a part in Rudolf's far-reaching schemes. Much the most important was annexation of the Tyrol (1363), whereby Rudolf energetically completed what his father had intelligently prepared, a significant link between the eastern and western Habsburg possessions. But at the same time Rudolf also reached out toward Friuli and Trent, Feltre and Belluno, as well as toward the Grisons, thus entering the northern Italian world of the city-states, whose early Renaissance princes he himself resembled. However, while he was staying in Milan with Bernabò Visconti—whom he had persuaded to launch a joint attack with him against the Patriarch of Aquileia and whose daughter Virida he had betrothed to his brother Leopold—a "raging fever" snatched the brilliant young Habsburg away from all his plans and ventures.

These were extraordinarily varied, even for so typical a

Renaissance figure. He invented a form of secret writing. He had the room in which he was born transformed into a chapel, and also fostered the cult of a St. Morandus, reportedly related to the early Habsburgs, as a dynastic saint. In his domestic edict of 1364, supposedly only a supplement to his father's but really intended to establish the prerogative of the eldest son, he was distinctly working for the principle of primogeniture. Many traits that we regard as typical of the Italian princes in the early Renaissance— the burning, uninhibited desire for fame; the efforts for external display of power and splendor; a circuitous political imagination, which often appears erratic and which encounters realities in a peculiar state of tension—were all highly developed in Rudolf IV.

Tension between the ideal and the real produces myth. From the tension between the actual renunciation of the crown after the Battle of Mühldorf, and the still vivid memory of the House's royal past, arose the myth of the special mission and election of the "Arch-house." Even though the word "Arch-house" did not appear for some time, it nevertheless stemmed from the title of *archidux*, archduke, first claimed by Rudolf IV, although established in the family only later. This archducal title was not a pure figment of the imagination, but came from the "extremely ancient" duchy of Carinthia. There the investiture of the duke took place, according to time-honored custom, on the *Zollfeld* (toll field),[3] which was regarded as proof that the ducal rank was rooted in native soil, and was independent of all higher power. Accordingly, during the period when the family was divided, only the branch that held Carinthia reassumed the archducal title (the first was Ernest the Iron Duke, father of Frederick III). Later, however, this special connection with Carinthia was lost, particularly after the

[3] Otto the Merry was the first Habsburg thus invested, in 1335.

Leopoldine line which carried the archducal title was the only one left to continue the House of Habsburg, in the the person of Maximilian. But even in Maximilian's *Wappenbuch* (book of heraldry) Carinthia is described as,

> . . . worshipful princes of Austria. These, first heathen and after- wards Christian, were always elected by the assembly of the Estates and then were awarded the duchy at the hands of a churl on a hill, who is called after his farm the king of "Zol," as a token that the Carinthians are subject to no one except the prince of their own country.

Because Frederick III (who in spite of a basically differ- ent personality from that of Rudolf IV revived many of his ideas and ambitions) when he was Emperor almost a century later authenticated the forged letters of independ- ence, they became valid imperial and domestic Habsburg law. To later Habsburgs the childless Rudolf bequeathed his faith in the mission and election of his House, along with the range of his political ambitions, which were fo- cused on Bohemia, Hungary, northern Italy, and the lands on both sides of the Upper Rhine, but above all on the kingship. Thus Rudolf IV stands between Albert I, his grandfather, and Frederick III, his grandnephew, in the midst of the "crownless" period, as founder of Habsburg mythology and transmitter of the family's belief in its right to the throne.

7: Dynasty Divided

Rudolf IV's efforts to extend his influence into northern Italy, cut off by his death, were made on the assumption that he had already protected his country against his more powerful neighbors to the north and east, Bohemia and Hungary. The treaties of succession concluded by the three ruling Houses at Brünn in 1364—which after later developments were often interpreted as having been the first preview of the Habsburg monarchy on the Danube—in reality represented a fairly thorough subordination of the Habsburgs to the more powerful Luxemburgers, whose prospects for succession to the Habsburgs' domains at that time were more favorable than those of the Habsburgs for succession in Bohemia or even in Hungary. The Brünn treaties of inheritance can be seen as fresh proof of the fact (already clear in the history of preceding centuries) that the three areas of the Alps, the Sudetenland, and the Carpathians, geopolitically and economically joined like a cloverleaf at the Vienna basin, have again and again invited attempts at closer political union.

All Rudolf's energy was needed to fuse into one unit of political power the complex of widely scattered lands under Habsburg control: Austria above and below the river Enns, Styria, Carinthia, Carniola, the Tyrol, the lands on the Upper Rhine and the possessions in Friuli; and to make the most of their widely diversified potentialities and challenges. But when Rudolf died in Milan in 1365, his two surviving brothers Albert and Leopold were fifteen and fourteen years old.

With the dynasty weakly represented, the separatist tendencies of the individual countries, whose political life was carried on by their own landed nobility, finally gained the ascendant. Since the initiative passed from dynastic rule, which unified the various lands under it, to the federalist principle, which grouped together individual countries, divisions of inheritance became inevitable in spite of the domestic edicts of Albert II and Rudolf IV. In addition, personal quarrels grew out of the fundamental differences of character between the quiet, almost shy Albert III and his warlike, splendor-loving, and power-hungry brother Leopold III. These two are almost models for the contrast between introvert and extrovert.

After several attempts to maintain—at least formally (as, for instance, in the allotment of income)—the joint rule decreed in the domestic edicts, a definite partition took place in 1379, the first since the separation of the branches of the family in 1239. Albert, the elder, received Upper and Lower Austria, lands overshadowed by the might of the Luxemburg dynasty. The remaining possessions, from which a far-reaching campaign along the lines of Rudolf IV's last ventures could be carried out, were received by Leopold. They were Styria, Carinthia, Carniola, and Tyrol (representing the base for a further thrust into Italy), as well as the patrimony on the Upper Rhine. This last—as Habsburg losses in those parts had proved in preceding periods—urgently required the support and prop of a larger domain, for which purpose only the Tyrol could be considered, because of its location. In these areas the Habsburgs succeeded, usually by peaceful means, in acquiring a few more significant possessions during the period just before and after the division of the family. The city of Freiburg in Breisgau, in its efforts to escape the control of the Counts of Freiburg, who were heavily in debt, allied itself earlier with the Habsburgs, then purchased its freedom for a very large sum in 1368 and placed itself under Habsburg sovereignty. In the south, Trieste, hard-pressed by Venice, finally sought protection with the Habsburgs in 1382.

Previously other territory in the regions of the Wendish March and Istria had been inherited from a cadet branch of the family of the Counts of Görz, and the county of Feldkirch, in the present Vorarlberg, had been purchased.

But Leopold III's policy of acquisition, which had moved entirely along the lines laid down by Rudolf IV, was suddenly interrupted in 1386 by a new catastrophe in the ancestral lands, the Battle of Sempach, in which Leopold's knights were wiped out by the Swiss Confederates and Duke Leopold himself was killed. He was buried in the monastery of Königsfelden, erected on the spot where the murder of 1308 had been committed. Again the life of an energetic Habsburg had come to a violent end in the ancestral lands. As his grandfather Albert's death in 1308 had signaled the decline of Habsburg power in what is now Switzerland, so Leopold's death marked not only a further milestone on this road but also the disappearance of the last possibility of halting, let alone reversing, the process.

During the next generation, under Leopold's youngest son Frederick IV of Tyrol, the founder of a new Leopoldine cadet branch (known in popular tradition as *"Friedel mit den leeren Taschen,"* Freddy of the empty pockets), the ruin of the ancestral Habsburg possessions became an accomplished fact. Since Frederick had helped Pope John XXIII[1] to escape from the Council-city of Constance, he was put under the ban of the Empire in 1415 and was declared to have forfeited his possessions. Aargau, the Habsburg heartland, was thereupon occupied by the Swiss Confederates; in Breisgau, the county of Badenweiler (mortgaged to the Habsburgs in 1398) was lost again, and the enemies of the Habsburgs in Breisgau and Switzerland concluded a firm alliance that set an in-

---

[1] This John XXIII (Baldassare Cossa), 1410–15, was involved in a triple schism and therefore is not counted in the official papal succession. For that reason it was possible for Cardinal Roncalli to become Pope John XXIII in 1958.

surmountable barrier to new Habsburg acquisitions in this area. When, after years of captivity, ban, and flight, Frederick had at least re-established his rule in the Tyrol, he tried in vain to acquire, in 1430, the old German imperial fief of Brabant, which may appear almost an anticipation of the later Habsburg acquisition of Burgundy. But the old ancestral lands on the Upper Rhine remained after 1415 a "political field of ruins" (Theodor Mayer); they did not become independent, but were administered from Innsbruck as "outlying districts," and parts of them were even mortgaged to the Duke of Burgundy.

The division into three branches—Albertine in Upper and Lower Austria, and two Leopoldine—determines Habsburg history in the fifteenth century. For in 1411, after the death of William and Leopold IV, the two older sons of Leopold III, his two surviving younger sons, Ernest "the Iron Duke"[2] and Frederick IV partitioned their lands anew. Ernest received Styria, Carinthia, and Carniola; Frederick, the Tyrol and the outlying districts. The splitting into three groups of territory was also based on geopolitical facts, since each group faced in a different direction for attack as well as defense. The Albertine lands, Upper and Lower Austria, faced Bohemia and Hungary, whose power-constellations helped decisively to determine the fate of the neighboring Austrian states, as, for instance, in the contemporary Hussite wars, which spilled across the northern borders into Austria. On the other hand, the fate of the central Austrian domain, belonging to the elder Leopoldine line, was more and more and more controlled by the regions on the southeastern frontier, southern Hungary and the northern parts of modern Yugoslavia—the territories threatened by the Turkish invasion.

In the fifteenth century (unlike the last decades of the fourteenth, when Leopold III concentrated his efforts at ex-

[2] The first to readopt the title of Archduke created by Rudolf IV, and also the first Habsburg to engage the Turks in battle, at Radkersburg in 1418.

pansion mainly on northern Italy, Friuli, and the Venetian plain), the Turkish threat from the southeast overshadowed all other political considerations and prompted a closer alliance between the elder Leopoldine branch and the Albertine one. The younger Leopoldine line in the Tyrol remained the principal champion of Habsburg western interests, as can be well seen from Frederick of Tyrol's vain efforts to obtain Brabant. However, it could not follow up the family's inherited interest in Italy as aggressively and successfully in the fifteenth century as in the fourteenth, because of the intra-Leopoldine division in 1411 and the elder branch's preoccupation with southeastern problems and the Turkish danger. That the whole House of Habsburg did not lose its feeling of solidarity in the tumultuous period of dynastic division and extremely unstable relations among the members of the various branches, can be at least partly credited to the regencies that were again and again taken over by members of one branch for minor rulers of another. But the struggle for these regencies, which were also claimed by the Diets of the respective areas, often weakened again the powers of the reigning sovereign.

The nadir of the ruler's impotence against the Diets and the apex of internal anarchy was finally reached under Frederick, the son of Ernest the Iron Duke and Cymburgis of Masovia, who was among Austrian Dukes the Fifth, among German Emperors the Third (or, if one recognizes and counts the disputed German kingship of Frederick the Handsome, the Fourth). Frederick III is undoubtedly one of the most problematic and peculiar, and certainly not one of the most attractive, figures in Habsburg history. Hardly any other Habsburg has been so ill-treated by historians, often undoubtedly for good reason, although the chivalrous judgment of the Swiss historian Jakob Burckhardt also contains some incontrovertible truth, "Much venomous comment on Frederick III is pure modern national liberalism. After four hundred years one tramples on a man who was helpless in his own time and sneers at anything that in the remotest past brought shame and sorrow to the House of Habsburg" *Historische Fragmente* (*Historic Fragments*).

A key to the understanding of Frederick's peculiar personality, to his failure as Austrian prince and as German Emperor, is perhaps provided by the entry in his diary where he says of the three great Habsburg defeats in the fourteenth century, Morgarten, Mühldorf, and Sempach, "*Das wainir von Oesterreich ist nit sigleich und mein vordern habent 3 streit darunder nidergelegen.*" ("The banner of Austria is not victorious and my forefathers suffered three defeats under it"). It was said of the elderly Emperor Francis Joseph that he did not love wars because he knew that one loses them—much the same attitude as that expressed by Frederick; in spite of all the great victories gained under Habsburg colors in every century, it represents a basic element in the political tradition of the House: a deep skepticism of the "fortunes of war" and a traditional love of peace; an awareness of the inevitability of war and conflict, always coupled with reluctance to entrust the fate of the House to the field of battle. This is surely also the core of wisdom in the proverb, usually so lightly and thoughtlessly quoted, "*Bella gerant alii, tu felix Austria nube*" (Let others fight wars, but you, happy Austria, marry), a cliché obviously at odds with the history of the House of Austria, rich in battles, tragic developments and decisions.

In Frederick III the political realism of the early Habsburgs develops into a sometimes almost pathological immobility, which sees the outliving of one's enemies as the chief aim of politics, and which could take as motto, Rilke's line "*Wer spricht von Siegen? Uebersteh'n ist alles*" (Who speaks of victories? Survival is everything). In the chaotic tangles of the waning Middle Ages, in the countless feuds that Frederick was involved in and that so often begot one another, in his struggles with the leaders of the powerful Estates, with the rebellious Viennese, with his own captains of mercenaries (who tried by force of arms to extract the pay constantly owing to them), in the wars with his own brother, Albert IV (so unlike him and so much more energetic), as much as in his role as emperor, Frederick carried to an extreme that policy of perseverance and survival that later became a basic Habsburg tenet.

More than just a phlegmatic attitude, and later adopted by Rudolf II, Leopold I, and Francis I in order to weather the storms of their times, in Frederick it was probably partly based on his almost cynical misanthropy, strong egoism, and deep-rooted conviction of the divine election of himself and his House, a belief apparently contradicted by his recognition of his own unstable position and the dangers threatening on all sides. For Habsburg rulers this belief in the election and mission of their House was probably a necessary supplement to their insights, the prop to which they clung all the more tenaciously the worse Fate treated them—and none clung more doggedly than Frederick III. However one interprets the famous five vowels, A.E.I.O.U., with which Frederick adorned all objects belonging to him and buildings erected by him, his use of the device indicates at any rate a strong awareness of his own importance and that of his House. Interpreted as *Austriae est imperare orbi universo* (*Alles Erdreich ist Oesterreich untertan*, the whole earth is subject to Austria), it was understood to mean, even before Frederick's time, that the House of Austria was rightfully entitled to the German royal and Roman imperial crowns. In this respect Frederick III was also the executor of Rudolf IV's political testament.

Frederick can properly be called the real founder of the Habsburg imperial position, which was not be be shaken again for three centuries. For the short reign (1437–39) of the next to the last Albertine, Albert V, son-in-law of the last

Luxemburg emperor Sigismund, is really an epilogue to Luxemburg rule rather than a prologue to a renewed rise of the Habsburgs, although the claims of the last Albertines, Albert V and his son Ladislas Posthumus, to sovereignty in Bohemia and Hungary were important for later Habsburg designs on these countries. With Albert V (as German king called Albert II), the dynasty had now achieved the crown again, more than a century after the murder of the first King Albert.

The election of Frederick III in 1440 must be understood in the light of the changed situation in Central Europe after the Luxemburg kingdom in Bohemia had been undermined by the Hussite troubles and the danger of the Turks. The prince electors called the Leopoldine Habsburg, the master of the southern borderlands, to the throne because of the Turkish peril, as well as the danger of new non-German centers of power coming into existence in eastern and central Europe. His task somewhat resembled that of his ancestor Rudolf when opposing Ottokar. Certainly, Emperor Frederick III cuts an even poorer figure when compared with Rudolf I. What Rudolf won from Ottokar, Frederick lost to the Hungarian kingdom of Mathias Corvinus; in Austria as in the Empire he was incapable of winning or even of holding his own. On the other hand, he was able to achieve what Rudolf had vainly striven for, coronation as emperor in Rome, albeit at the hands of a pope whose political power was much diminished. He was the last German ruler, and the only Habsburg in history, to enjoy this distinction. In Rome he married the Portuguese princess Eleanor who, having grown up in the splendor of late-medieval Portugal, must have felt like an outcast in the narrow and all too often miserable conditions of the Austrian duchy in those days, and who passed on her ambition for princely glory and world eminence to her son Maximilian.

Wherever possible, Frederick III avoided engaging in battle to achieve political ends; he preferred to let others do it. His strength lay in the persistent and patient spinning of political threads, which, broken and then knotted again and again, finally wove a net that ensnared many of his enemies and protected him from crashing into the abyss. As one studies Frederick's personality the picture of the patient spider, lying in wait for its victim, suggests itself again and again and, since spiders are usually regarded with horror and disgust, it is not surprising that Frederick has found few champions in later ages. From the point of view of Habsburg history, however, he is highly significant, not least because he persisted in all his claims with incredible tenacity, even at moments when they appeared to be totally illusory and worthless because of the actual balance of power. In west and east alike he maintained or himself created the basis for the future rise of his House, though probably he himself was not aware of the eventual consequences. At last, having survived all his enemies, he was able to watch his son Maximilian, so unlike himself, unify the divided possessions of all the Hapsburg branches and, as husband and heir of Mary of Burgundy, lead the House of Habsburg from helplessness to world power.

8: *The "House of Austria and Burgundy"*

Until the Habsburgs were invested with Austria, their family names, above all Rudolf and Albert, were those customarily used in their Alamannian home. After 1282, two of Albert I's sons received the Babenberg names of Frederick and Leopold. John, on the other hand, because of the parricide, was naturally shunned for centuries. The warlike and chivalric Leopold III, the "flower of knighthood," christened two of his sons William and Ernest, names derived from late medieval chivalric romances, though Ernest in turn reverted to the traditional Frederick and Albert for his sons. Therefore Maximilian, completely new in the family and rather unusual in its time, as the name of Frederick III's son, is an outward sign of the beginning of a new chapter in Habsburg history.

The biography of Maximilian as Emperor, dictated by himself, says that his mother, Eleanor of Portugal, proposed to call him Constantine, after the first Christian Emperor and ruler over Rome and Byzantium, while his father favored George, after the knightly saint who fought against the heathen. But the baby's godfather, Nicholas of Ujlak, a Hungarian-Croat magnate who had fought under Janos Hunyadi against the Turks, asked to choose a name that had some relation to his campaigns, and proposed as patron Maximilian of Cilli, saint, martyr, and champion in the struggle against the Turks. Eleanor's besetting idea that her son was predestined to be a new Constantine was already evident at the time of her marriage in Rome, when she obtained permission from Pope Nicholas to change her name from Leonora (unusual in German countries) to Helen, the name of Constantine's mother. Thus she would bear an auspicious name like her husband (who interpreted his name as meaning "rich in peace").

The christening of Maximilian expresses not only his mother's high hopes for her only son, but also the Habsburg interest in the southeast; however, the destiny of the boy who, at thirteen, had been besieged with his imperial family in the Viennese *Hofburg* (both palace and castle) by his uncle Albert VI and the rebellious Viennese, lay not in eastern but in western Europe. He was fourteen when he first met the resplendent Charles the Bold, Duke of Burgundy, in his father's retinue, and eighteen when he married Charles's daughter Mary of Burgundy, Europe's richest heiress. What the Habsburgs had been attempting for two centuries, but had never achieved (Rudolf I through his policy of acquiring land on the Upper Rhine before he became king; Albert I through his plan of adding Holland to his House; Rudolf IV through his claim to the title of "Duke of Swabia"; Frederick of Tyrol through his attempted annexation of Brabant), the possession of a great western European domain, fell to the share of young Maximilian, and in a measure far exceeding all earlier plans and even the boldest hopes.

The acquisition of Burgundy determined the destiny and way of life of the Habsburg dynasty in the coming epoch. This is clearly reflected in the new family names. The son of Maximilian and Mary was named for Charles the Bold's father, Philip the Good; their daughter was named for Charles's second wife, Margaret of York; and Maximilian's grandson was called Charles. The old Burgundian rivalry with the French reigning House of Valois, arising from the hostility of a cadet branch to the major line, was henceforth a decisive and constant element in Habsburg policy, until Marie Antoinette's marriage to the Dauphin. The Habsburgs also inherited a wide-ranging system of alliances with the other enemies of France—England, Spain, and Savoy. For English pay, Maximilian (combining his own interests with those of his employers) carried on the fight against the House of Valois, while his ties with Spain (the double marriage of his children, Philip and Margaret, to John and Joanna, children of the Spanish king) led, by a series of unpredictable events, to Habsburg world power under Charles V. The formation of this global Empire took place within the framework of the anti-French system built up by Charles the Bold. Hostility to France also reawoke Habsburg interest in Italy, which had become the second major battlefield after the Netherlands in the struggle against France. Finally, the acquisition of Burgundy and its traditional feud gave additional significance to the position of the Habsburgs within the Empire. As they had protected the eastern Empire against the Turks through the Austrian hereditary lands and later through the acquisition of Hungary, so as heirs of Burgundy they took over the protection of the western Empire; the Habsburg lands enclosed and shielded the Empire just as a turtle's shell encloses its body.

For the House of Habsburg itself the Burgundian marriage of 1477 meant a return to the great political drama played by the western European dynasties, in which the Habsburgs after Albert I's death had gradually ceased to figure importantly. It meant also a shift in stress from east to west, and thus the halting of the eastward movement that had dominated Habsburg policy from King Rudolf's fight against Ottokar down to Frederick III and Maximilian. Since dynastic marriages can be regarded as an indication of political interests, the return to the west began with Frederick III's choice of a Portuguese wife. Marriages into western European ruling Houses had last taken place among King Albert I's sons (the wife of the unfortunate Frederick the Handsome had been a princess of Aragon); after Rudolf IV, marriages into Houses with eastern domains, especially the House of Luxemburg, predominated, while Leopold III's marriage to Virida Visconti expressed the dynasty's interest in northern

Italy. Albert III, for example, was first married to a Luxemburg princess, then tried in vain to win the hand of a Visconti, and finally took to wife a Hohenzollern, daughter of the Burgrave of Nürnberg. Frederick III's father, Ernest the Iron Duke, was first married to a Pomeranian princess and then to Cymburgis of Masovia (in modern Poland), while Albert V chose a Luxemburg wife.

With Maximilian, the imaginative and volatile son of a Portuguese princess (Charles the Bold's mother was also Portuguese), the House of Habsburg took cultural and intellectual root in the Burgundian world. Maximilian wrote to his children in French (the first instance of the extraordinary Habsburg gift for languages, kept alive and strengthened through constant use, which enabled them to live among and rule people of many different nationalities); the late medieval Order of the Knights of the Golden Fleece became the great order of the House of Habsburg; in fact, Habsburg court ceremonial, later called "Spanish," was originally Burgundian. Thus the Burgundian "waning of the Middle Ages" was transformed, without interruption, into the splendor of the Habsburg global Empire at the beginning of the modern period. The "House of Austria" became the *Maison d'Autriche*," the "House of Austria and Burgundy," as Maximilian first called his family. As Albert I had brought Alamannian vassals to Austria, so Maximilian now formed his retinue from the great and noble families of Burgundy and the Netherlands, with their mixed French and Flemish culture. This connection with the cultural and intellectual world of France and the Netherlands became immeasurably important for the entire future development of civilization in the eastern European countries, just as, later and on a much smaller scale, the link with the west through the inheritance of Mark-Cleves on the Lower Rhine became important to Brandenburg-Prussia.

Maximilian not only garnered the rich Burgundian inheritance, which he defended in fierce struggles against the French kings and the self-confident burghers of the Flemish cities—he was also the first Habsburg to unite the lands of all the branches of the family under one ruler. In this he was decisively helped by the fact that Sigismund of Tyrol ("Moneybags"), who had no legitimate heirs and under whose rule more Habsburg ancestral land had been lost to the Swiss Confederates, transferred his lands to Maximilian. With their financial reserves, especially the income from the Tyrolean silver mines, he was able to regain the eastern territories lost to Hungary.

From Sigismund he also inherited the very important connection with the Fugger banking house, without whose financial help a ruler constantly short of cash could not have carried out his numerous wars and enterprises. The unification of the lands of both Leopoldine branches (completed under Maximilian by inheritance of the "outermost county" around Lienz, after the extinction of that line of the Counts of Görz in 1500) enabled him be begin an aggressive Italian policy again, like that of Rudolf IV and Leopold III, which now, because of the French king's designs on Italy, became subsumed in the greater contest with France.

Maximilian's second marriage, with Bianca Maria Sforza of Milan, his war with Venice (during which he held Verona for a considerable time), and finally the establishment of a southern border to the Empire that lasted for centuries, were the most important achievements of his Italian policy. But as heir of the Tyrolean branch of the family Maximilian also continued his House's traditional interest in the southwest, by waging a last war against the Swiss, and by repossessing in 1504 the Tyrolean districts of Kufstein, Kitzbühel, and Rattenberg that had been ceded to Bavaria in 1369. In his later years the Tyrol came to be the favorite part of his vast dominion. In its mountains he loved to hunt chamois (hunting, incidentally, remained the great Habsburg passion down to

Francis Joseph and Francis Ferdinand), and in its capital he built his enormous tomb, though he was actually never buried in it. Even as a fragment it is an impressive testimony to his belief in the glory and the divine election of his House.

As heir of the Albertine branch, Maximilian urged the claims to Bohemia and Hungary so stubbornly maintained by his father Frederick, and renewed them through the double marriage of his grandchildren, Ferdinand and Mary, to the children of Vladislav, Jagellon king of Bohemia and Hungary, at the congress of princes in Vienna in 1515. The temporary opposition of Vladislav's brother, King Sigismund of Poland, to these plans led to Maximilian's contact with the Tsar of Russia, who was at war with Sigismund.

The extraordinary span of Maximilian's policy of marriages and alliances, reaching from Spain and England to Hungary and Russia (once he even considered presenting himself as as a candidate for the Swedish throne), is partly explained by his inheritance of all the widely diversified claims and aspirations of the three different branches of the family. The breadth of his political plans corresponded to the volatility of his imaginative and unsteady nature, so that when, after his first wife's death, he wanted to marry the heiress of Brittany, his father Frederick reproached him for his "disreputable imbroglios," which had neither rhyme nor reason.

One is accustomed to regard Maximilian's restlessness and his inconsistency—almost caprice—as expressing the *Zeitgeist* of the "transition period" from Middle Ages to modern times (as in the classic professorial howler, "With one foot Maximilian stood in the Middle Ages, and with the other he hailed the rising sun of modern times"), and it is frequently pointed out that the "last knight" was also the first foot soldier and artilleryman. To be sure, the period around 1500 was one of great unrest, important changes, and the collision of great historic antitheses—but every period in history is a time of transition, in which the old dies off and ground is prepared for the new. That Maximilian took up all the interests of his age, even when they were contradictory, that he was so very alive to all its plans, ideas, possibilities, and developments, and that he reacted instantly to each challenge, no matter whence it came, may possibly be due to his heredity. His parents were completely unlike each other, and in his family tree we find members of all the different European nations, so that the genes of his German, Italian, Polish, and Portuguese ancestors perhaps maintained his personality in a continual state of tension, unable to find harmony and balance.

But the tension created by the period and by Maximilian's parentage was above all geopolitical. In many respects he reminds one of Rudolf IV. Besides the common family tradition and the—somewhat remote—common ancestry, they had common political tasks. Rudolf IV was the last Habsburg before the division of the family, as Maximilian was the first after it. But for the great-grandnephew an even greater tension existed between the variety and scope of the tasks that offered, in fact even urged, themselves upon him, and the limitation of his material means; this occasionally gave his policy, more than that of Rudolf IV, a fantastic and unreal quality. However, both Rudolf and Maximilian proved again and again that they were by no means dreamers, but men of exceptional political gifts. Above all, Maximilian possessed outstanding talents for negotiation, which helped him in many difficult situations, and also an intuitive understanding of the importance of political propaganda. The tension among his various inherited strains certainly helped him to think himself into the role of his partner in negotiation or the target of his propaganda and, whether dealing with German burghers, Burgundian nobles, Italian princes, or eastern European kings, he was able always to address a kindred element.

As the healer of divisions in his family, Maximilian strove to interconnect the inherited domains more closely. He planned, though he did not achieve, a kingdom of "Austria and Burgundy"; he started a central Habsburg administration with the idea of yoking the countries together and overcoming the separatist tendencies promoted by the local Diets. Burgundian administration probably provided a model, but the decisive impetus came from his desire to restrict the power of the Diets and to gather all financial and military resources together in the ruler's own hand.

For the same reasons Maximilian also tried to carry out an imperial reform and to create a strong German monarchy, and sought to give it higher sanction by adopting the title of "Roman Emperor Elect," independent of the coronation in Rome. Frederick III's reign, quite apart from the limitations imposed on it by his character, had demonstated that a small southeast-German territory was not an adequate base for a really powerful, not merely nominal, German monarchy. Now that this basis of power had been greatly enlarged and extended, Maximilian was the first Habsburg ruler since King Albert's death who could attempt to build a strong German monarchy. But the development of almost two centuries could not be annihilated. The Emperor's reform was now opposed by the Empire itself, by the entire imperial Diet under the leadership of the Elector of Mainz, Berthold of Henneberg; German constitutional development thus remained suspended in this dualism of "Emperor and Empire." After a century and a half of struggle between the Emperor's "monarchic" and the Diet's "aristocratic" concepts of the fountainhead of imperial power, the Peace of Westphalia legally established a compromise.

Even if Maximilian did not succeed with his imperial reform, in creating the imperial supreme court (*Reichsgericht*), setting up administrative districts, and instituting military and tax reforms, he founded an organization that met the most urgent requirements. He was the German Renaissance ruler *par excellence*, the Maecenas of German artists, and the friend of the south German upper bourgeoisie, especially in Augsburg and Nürnberg. Here he resembled his ancestor Rudolf I, and like him he was well commemorated in popular tradition. As head and center of a group of German humanists, he promoted a conscious German nationalism that was stimulated by the descriptions of the Germanic tribes in Caesar and Tacitus; he exploited nationalism and patriotism in the fight against France, and he ordered a collection to be made of old German sagas and heroic songs. The German nationalism that he displayed at the imperial Diets and in his dealings with the German bourgeoisie, in his speeches, and in his political propaganda, was always inseparable from his belief in his House and its mission to rule Christendom.

Hence his dynastic-political and genealogical ideas—reflected alike in the design for his splendid Innsbruck tomb and in the books, genealogies, and pictures that he inspired —were much more than the idle trifles of a luxury-loving and vainglorious ruler. Maximilian clearly preferred the Franco-Trojan to the Roman patrician legend of his family's descent, because it expressed the new western orientation of Habsburg policy and demonstrated his superiority to the French royal House, because of his alleged descent from the Merovingians. At the same time, by claiming descent through Priam from the Trojans, he showed that his German family was equal, if not superior, to the Romans, whose Trojan descent stemmed only from Aeneas. Priam's supposed journey from Troy through Austria to the Rhine established a providential connection with the Habsburg ancestral lands. Finally, since European humanism considered Greek antiquity the expression of the highest nobility, the link with Troy (predecessor of Constantinople) also suggested Byzantium, entirely conforming to the ideas of Maximilian's mother when she wished to name her son Constantine.

There is not too wide a gap between these notions and the fantastic plans of the old Emperor, widowed for the second time, to become papal Coadjutor and finally Pope himself, thus combining the two highest dignities of Christendom either in his own person, or at least in his dynasty. When Maximilian developed the idea and wrote that Ferdinand of Aragon favored the project on condition that the imperial crown be bestowed on their common grandson, Charles, it was part of a famous humorous letter to his daughter Margaret, in which he remarked that he very much hoped to become a saint after his death and should be very proud to have her pray to him when she was in distress. But unquestionably he really did consider acquiring the tiara. It has been suggested that his sole motive was to lay hands on the Curia's large income, a theory that cannot be entirely dismissed in view of Maximilian's permanent lack of funds. But the genealogical works he inspired prove that he was also influenced by his convinced belief in the predestination of his House to the highest offices in Christendom. The impressive illustrations in Jakob Mennel's *Fürstlich Cronickh kayser Maximilians geburtsspiegel* (*Princely chronicle of Emperor Maximilian's genealogical mirror*), and its companion the illuminated manuscript *Kaiser Maximilians besonder Buch genannt der Zaiger* (*Emperor Maximilian's particular book, called the Pointer* [also clock hand]) exemplify the orientation of all Habsburg history and genealogy toward Empire and Papacy.

9: Habsburg World Power

Maximilian partly achieved and partly far surpassed Rudolf IV's dreams and aspirations for his House. Though Maximilian, by his policy of alliances and marriages, prepared the ground for the House's increase in power under his grandsons Charles V and Ferdinand I, he still could not possibly have foreseen what an unexpectedly rich harvest it would bring in. The further rise of the Habsburgs had something mysterious about it, especially for contemporaries: first the addition of the Spanish inheritance—just then enormously increased in wealth and influence through the discovery of the fabulous transatlantic countries; in eastern Europe the establishment of the claim to the Hungarian and Bohemian crowns; in Central Europe the acquisition of Württemberg; and finally the election of Charles as Emperor.

The Habsburg belief in the mission and election of their House seemed brilliantly confirmed, and God's blessing appeared visibly to rest on it. Members of the newly successful House led the great movement for purifying and renewing the Church that was stirring all Christendom, and later (after the resulting schism) led in the attempt to bridge the religious division as well as to defend Christendom against the Turks. In this important hour for world history, however, the House's destiny lay with two of Maximilian's grandsons, offspring of Philip, who had died young, and his wife, the insane Spanish Princess Joanna.

Charles and Ferdinand, in spite of occasional strained relations over questions of policy, allocation of rule, and succession, as well as the inevitable division of inheritance, worked well together and their personalities complemented each other. They were able to provide a model, according to the precepts in the older Habsburg domestic edicts, which later generations could follow even if they did not always choose to do so. The co-operation and preservation of good form, even in violent disagreements, were all the more estimable since the brothers were not only quite different in character and inclinations, but had also spent their childhood apart—Ferdinand in Spain and Charles in the Netherlands. Nor were Spanish efforts lacking to realize the wish of the brothers' Spanish grandfather, Ferdinand of Aragon, that the younger Ferdinand should rule Spain.

Perhaps the brothers and sisters (who must also be included, particularly the queens Eleanor of Portugal—later of France—and Mary, widow of Louis of Hungary) got on so well together because, after their father's early death and their mother's insanity, they grew up as orphans. Conscious of their singular dynastic situation and of their lonely distinction, they felt especially dependent on each other. The many struggles in which Charles and Ferdinand were repeatedly involved and which basically contradicted their peace-loving natures, and their constant and only too well-founded fear of treachery and deceit in their immediate entourage, may also in the end have helped the two Habsburgs to settle all their differences peacefully.

Among the people who trained the two young princes in the traditions of their dynasty, who formed their image of the world, and who educated them as rulers, the most important for Charles was the Archduchess Margaret. She was Maximilian's daughter and confidante, already twice widowed at twenty-four. In intellectual capacity, love of the arts, diplomatic acumen, and healthy, ironic sense of humor, she very much resembled her father. Maximilian not only could take a joke but could even make fun of his constant pecuniary difficulties, his passion for hunting, and his genealogical interests, and in this Margaret proved herself his equal. At seventeen, while crossing to Spain to meet the Spanish *infante* John, who had been married to her by proxy, she was caught in a terrible storm in the Bay of Biscay. She had a small bag of gold coins tied to her hand for a princely burial, together with a strip of parchment on which —alluding to her marriage at the age of three and her repudiation at eleven by Charles VIII of France—she had written:

> *Cy-gist Margot, la gentil' demoiselle*
> *Qu'ha deux marys et encore est pucelle.*
>
> (*Here lies Margot, the demoiselle,*
> *Twice married but a virgin still.*)

Margaret also composed very beautiful and deeply felt French poems about the fickleness of human fortune, and built the exquisite church in Bourg-en-Bresse as a unique monument to her short happiness as Philip of Savoy's consort. This intelligent Regent of the Netherlands, who enchanted her contemporaries as much as she has her later biographers, also takes her place in the long series of remarkable Habsburg women who, as regents over individual parts of the widely scattered domains, wise counselors of the rulers, and patient mediators among the male members of the House, played important roles at different times, though usually the details are obscure.

Charles—born at Ghent in 1500 and named for his great-grandfather, the last Duke of Burgundy—was, even more than his grandfather Maximilian, entirely at home in the world of Burgundy and the Netherlands. The Habsburg domains in the southeast held hardly any associations for him. The courtly and dynastic ideas and the chivalric traditions of the Burgundian Late Middle Ages determined his character at first, but he responded also to another important environmental influence, a deep and earnest piety, stemming from the Netherlands tradition of the *devotio moderna*, which was communicated to him by his teacher, Adrian of Utrecht, later Pope Hadrian VI.

Here a new religious element entered into Habsburg family tradition, significantly at a time when the House had so miraculously, over and beyond all other ruling dynasties, assumed the leadership of Christendom, and when the problems of maintaining ecclesiastical unity and of reforming the Church body and soul were more urgent than anyone could have imagined. To be sure, the earlier Habsburgs too had been pious in a general way; following the example of their ancestor Rudolf, they had always striven to keep on good terms with the Papacy, they had founded churches and monasteries, and had endowed masses and collected relics. But in all this they had hardly differed from the other ruling families of Europe during the late Middle Ages. Now, when other dynasties were increasingly influenced by Renaissance secular motives and reasons of state, the "House of Austria and Burgundy," rooted in the Netherlands, significantly became imbued with a new piety, conceived as a strict personal obligation.

Frequently the later alliance of the Habsburgs with the Counter Reformation—and with its ecclesiastical exponents and representatives, the Jesuits—has been reflected back to Charles and Ferdinand, thus blurring the peculiar nuances of Habsburg piety and ecclesiastical policy. They were principally indebted to the spirit of Erasmus of Rotterdam, the great scholar and humanist, who exercised a lasting influence on both brothers, but perhaps even more on Charles than on Ferdinand. Charles's untiring attempts to settle the schism peacefully, and to convene a universal council; Ferdinand's concessions—undoubtedly also conditioned by power politics—to the reformers; and finally the unequivocal Protestant sympathies of Ferdinand's son, Maximilian, all sprang from the basic attitude determined by Erasmus. But even the spiritual and religious climate under Philip II showed clearly that the spirit of Erasmus had not yet died, for Erasmus appealed strongly to Spaniards. His work on the Christian prince became the handbook for educating Habsburg children.

The difficulties that Charles V and his son Philip II, as the most powerful rulers in Italy, had with the Papacy, which repeatedly and almost inevitably opposed them in politics, reinforced Habsburg independence. So did their continuing belief in the special consecration of the ruler. As steward and protector of the Church, he had the right and the duty to supervise it and suppress abuses. For the Habsburgs the system and philosophy of a state church (later called *Josephinismus*, after the ruler who governed during the period of its most intense development and its spiritual, if not yet formal, separation from its religious basis) grew organically out of the medieval tradition. As the Habsburg concept of the Emperor, expressed most grandiosely under Charles V, again approached the imperial idea of the Hohenstaufens, relations with the Papacy were almost inevitably strained. In modern times, the history of the Habsburgs—most faithful sons of the Catholic Church and legitimate heirs of the "Catholic Kings" and defenders of the faith in Spain—is also the history of almost uninterrupted conflicts with the Roman Curia.

The central motive power in Charles V's thought and action was the concept of the Emperor, the noble idea of the imperial office as the highest sovereign dignity of Christendom, inextricably bound up with the concept of his House. These ideas explain and connect all his governmental measures, military campaigns, and diplomatic negotiations: the defense against the Turks, the campaigns against Algiers and Tunisia, the conflicts and co-operation with the Papacy, the struggle with the French royal House and the almost realized plan to acquire England for the House of Habsburg through

Philip's marriage to Mary Tudor, the fight with the German Protestant princes, and finally also his abdication. Religion cannot be distinguished from politics in these closely interwoven ventures, battles, and plans, just as the concept of the Emperor cannot be separated from the interests of the House of Habsburg.

Probably Charles's counselors contributed decisively to his concept of the Emperor; the strongest influence was that of the Lord Chancellor, Mercurino Gattinara, a Piedmontese from Vercelli, who lived entirely in the intellectual and spiritual world of Dante's *De Monarchia*. But as grandson of Maximilian and pupil of the Archduchess Margaret, Charles derived from his family upbringing a vivid idea of the dignity and dedication of the imperial office. When Charles harshly rejected his brother Ferdinand's suggested candidacy for election in the Empire, and when he disputed with the Spaniards, who had taken umbrage at the precedence of the Roman over the Spanish royal title, he clearly formulated his concept of the imperial office as a dignity far outranking and outshining all other royal and sovereign titles. The office of Roman Emperor was the highest dignity established by God on earth, and, according to a decree issued in Barcelona on September 5, 1519, which settled the quarrel over the title, he called himself:

Don Carlos, by the Grace of God King of the Romans, future and always sublime Emperor, King of Castile, of Léon, of both Sicilies, of Jerusalem, of Granada, of Navarre, of Toledo, of Valencia, of Galicia, of Mallorca, of Seville, of Sardinia, of Cordova, of Corsica, of Murcia, of Jaén, of Algarve, of Algeciras, of Gibraltar, of the Canary Islands, of the lands in the ocean sea, Archduke of Austria, Duke of Burgundy and of Brabant, Count of Barcelona and of Flanders and of the Tyrol, Lord of Biscay and of Molina, Duke of Athens and of Neopatria, Count of Roussillon and of Cerdena, Marquis of Oristan and Gociano.

Considerations of empire as well as family lent great importance to the manner of settling the younger brother

Ferdinand's claims to the inheritance. The Habsburg principle of collective inheritance, valid in the Habsburg domains,
was confronted by the principle of primogeniture prevailing
in the rest of western Europe. The multiple tasks involved
in ruling the Empire, Austria, and Burgundy, scarcely man-
ageable even in Maximilian's time, were now still further
complicated by the inheritance of the Spanish kingdoms.
Like the Habsburg domains they possessed highly divergent
traditions and tendencies. Under Ferdinand and Isabella the
kingdoms had been joined only through a sort of "matri-
monial union," the marriage of their rulers, the "Catholic
Kings." Their daughter, Joanna, and then her son, Charles
(who ruled in his insane mother's name as well as in his own),
were the first rulers of a united Spanish realm, whose individual parts not only preserved the titles of independent
kingdoms, but also for a long time, in some cases even until
the present day, kept their own pronounced individuality.
Castile, facing the Atlantic, protagonist in overseas explora-
tions and conquests, was allied with Portugal—ruled by a
much interrelated and intermarried dynasty—as well as with
the other countries of the Atlantic coast, above all with the
Netherlands, and politically and economically also with
England. Aragon, on the other hand, belonged to the Mediterranean polity, and had successfully grasped at Sicily and
southern Italy, where it had come into contact with the
Habsburg interest in northern Italy. Common to both
Spanish groups of territories was their enmity for France,
which also linked them to the Netherlands as well as to
the traditional Leopoldine policy of expansion into northern
Italy. Since the French king, Francis I, had competed for
the imperial crown, and had then allied himself against the
Habsburgs with the Protestant German princes, and even
with the Turks, the quarrel between the Houses of Habsburg
and Valois was also an integral part of Charles V's efforts
to maintain religious unity and to protect Christendom

against its internal and external foes, heretics, and infidels.

The fight against the enemies of Christendom and for the propagation of the Faith, foremost aims in Charles the Bold's and Maximilian's world of courtly and chivalric ideas, had preoccupied the Spanish kingdoms for centuries. When the world of the Burgundian Order of the Golden Fleece joined that of the Spanish chivalric orders of Santiago, Alcántara, and Calatrava (whose Grand Master Charles V also became), it merged with the traditions of the Spanish *reconquista* and the Spanish consciousness of mission and election (which had been hardened in contest with the Moors). The Burgundian court ceremonial became Burgundian-Spanish.

A curious picture therefore emerges of the whole complex of lands governed by the House of Habsburg at the beginning of the sixteenth century. Everywhere the old-established and widely divergent traditions of the subject kingdoms and territories were alive, but were fitted into a grand system, spanning the whole of Christendom, so that they were enriched, intensified, and sometimes even disciplined. When Charles fought in Italy he continued the traditions of both his grandfathers, Maximilian and Ferdinand of Aragon, while at the same time acting as the legitimate heir of the Ghibelline imperial policy of the High Middle Ages. When he attempted, through the English marriage of his son, to incorporate England more closely in the anti-French system of alliances, he followed the Burgundian and Castilian traditions as well as the teachings of his aunt Margaret, who, as Regent of the Netherlands, had followed a decidedly anglophile policy, conforming to an Anglo-Burgundian tradition. If his English plans had succeeded, they would have been at the same time the culmination of his imperial policy.

The vast geographic scope and diversity of the Habsburg territories immeasurably intensified the old problem of east-west tension. Though the Spanish inheritance shifted the balance of Habsburg sovereignty farther west, a more active policy in the east seemed both opportune and necessary. But the concrete east-west problem facing the brothers was the difference between western and east-central European laws of inheritance, between primogeniture and collective inheritance. This became the crucial question and the great test of strength for the concept of the House and also for that of the Emperor.

As early as 1521, during the first imperial Diet that young King Charles—greeted with great hope in Germany—held at Worms (where he first encountered the new doctrine in the person of Luther), a first treaty of partition between Charles and Ferdinand had been concluded. Ferdinand—whose hopes of succeeding to the Spanish inheritance, in the westernmost corner of the Habsburg domain, had recently been raised by courtiers and flatterers—was to be compensated with the easternmost part and was to receive only the five Austrian duchies (Austria above and below the Enns, Styria, Carinthia, and Carniola), while Charles was to get the rest: Spain, the multifarious Burgundian inheritance, the Habsburg patrimony on the Upper Rhine, the Tyrol, and the whole ring of possessions in northern Italy and Friuli down to Trieste and Istria.

The fundamental purpose of this plan of partition is clear. The ruler of the Empire was to be able to rely on a German base (the Tyrol and the lands below the Alps), and he was to keep in his own hands the important Brenner Pass to Italy and all territories that could serve as points of departure for Italian campaigns. But immediately legal difficulties arose, since by legal precedent the Görz-Friuli possessions belonged to the eastern group of countries, Carinthia and Carniola. Probably even more important was the consideration that a new division of the Austrian lands might easily weaken the Habsburg position in the Empire, and also that Ferdinand, when once he pressed his claims to Bohemia and Hungary,

would need the support of all the Habsburg territory. Moreover, in spite of all his apparent willingness to yield to
Charles (about which Ferdinand's son, Maximilian II, complained later) Ferdinand, the more lively and charming of
the two brothers, also possessed a certain toughness and
obstinacy in negotiation comparable to that of his grandfather Maximilian, who, though volatile, repeatedly seized a
good opportunity to return stubbornly to his favorite ideas.

As early as the following year a new division of the inheritance was arranged in Brussels. Here Ferdinand received the
entire "dominion over Austria" from Alsace to the Hungarian border, while Charles, besides the imperial crown and
the Spanish kingdoms with their Italian dependencies, retained only the Burgundian inheritance. However, this agreement was at first to be kept secret, and for the time being
Ferdinand was to be officially regarded as his brother's vice-
regent in the southern Austrian lands ceded to him, in the
Tyrol, and in Germany north of the Alps, including Württemberg. In Alsace, Pfirt, and Hagenau Ferdinand was to rule
only during his own lifetime; after his death they were to
revert to Burgundy, and thus to Charles or his descendants.
Ferdinand on his part renounced all heritable claims to the
Burgundian and Spanish lands. The treaty was not to be
published for six years, or till the date of Charles's imperial
coronation, which was to be followed by Ferdinand's election
as King of the Romans.

This Brussels treaty of 1522 became enormously significant for Habsburg and European history. The old Habsburg
estates provided Ferdinand and his descendants with a strong
base for the later acquisition of Bohemia and Hungary and
for the imperial succession. It had been decided that suppos-
ing both brothers were to have male heirs (as they did in
fact, though this was by no means certain when the Treaty
of Brussels was concluded), the House of Habsburg, at that
time whole and entire, would split into Spanish and German,

not Burgundian and Hungarian, branches (which would have been the result of the first Worms treaty). When considering the House as a whole, the Treaty of Brussels made due allowances for the shift of balance to the west.

More than two decades later, Charles tried vainly to alter the Brussels decision in favor of his own son Philip, who had been born and had grown up in the interval. It was rumored that the Emperor intended to help his own son, instead of Ferdinand, to the imperial succession. Ferdinand's violent reaction to such rumors as he had heard made these plans—if indeed they were ever seriously considered—unrealizable, quite apart from the German princes' obvious distaste for Philip. At that time, the heavy strain on the good relations between Charles and Philip on the one hand, and Ferdinand and his son Maximilian on the other, could be relieved only during protracted and difficult negotiations in Augsburg, and through the intelligent mediation of the Queen Dowager Mary of Hungary, sister to Charles and Ferdinand.

The resulting compromise provided that succession to the imperial office alternate between the two branches. Charles was to be followed by Ferdinand, he in turn by Philip, and he again by Ferdinand's son Maximilian. Charles clearly was attempting to safeguard, by almost desperate means, the unity of "our House." But Ferdinand at that time already spoke and thought of "our Houses." Whether he ever seriously intended to keep his promise to Charles that, after becoming Emperor, he would work for Philip's election as King of the Romans, and thereafter as designated Emperor, must remain an open question.

His brother's resistance to Charles's plans for the succession, together with setbacks in other spheres (the quarrels with the Protestant German princes and with France; the German developments that led to the Religious Peace of Augsburg in 1555—not approved by the Emperor; the failure

of the plans made for the acquisition of England, because of
Queen Mary's childlessness; the death of the Emperor's insane mother, Joanna; and finally his own weakened health)
all persuaded Charles to resign his crowns and offices and to
withdraw from the struggles of this world. Moving even to
the modern reader is Charles's magnificent description of the
events at the turn of the year [1555–56], in which he first
resigned the Mastership of the Order of the Golden Fleece,
then the lordship of the Netherlands, and almost three
months later that of Castile, Aragon, Sicily, and the New
World, and the Grand Mastership of the three Spanish
chivalric orders of Santiago, Alcántara, and Calatrava.

The impression made by the abdication of the Emperor,
of all western rulers since Charlemagne closest to the late
Roman ideal of the universal ruler, was particularly deep and
lasting on contemporaries and later generations. This explains the persistent but inaccurate notion that after his
abdication he withdrew to a monastery as a simple monk.
In reality he spent his last years in an imperial villa, specially
built for him, adjoining the monastery of San Jeronimo de
Yuste; up to his last hours he was kept informed about all
important political developments, and was again and again
asked for advice by his children and former assistants. He
was also occupied to the end with family matters, such as
the problem of securing Habsburg hereditary succession in
Portugal if the minor Infante Don Sebastian were to die
prematurely. (In the event, Philip II took over Portugal in
1580, after the bold and visionary Don Sebastian—who had
passionately adopted the ideas of his Portuguese, Spanish,
Burgundian, and Habsburg ancestors on crusades and battles
against the infidel—lost his life in a North African campaign.)

With Charles V and his imperial administration the House
of Habsburg rose to heights never achieved before or since.
The range of the territories governed, the grandeur of the
global conflicts, ventures, and plans, corresponded to the

Emperor's majestic and noble manner of life, which was at the same time utterly plain and devoid of all hollow pomp, and matched the august dignity of his appearance—not perhaps conventionally attractive, but deeply impressive—which Titian's brush has preserved for us in unchanging vitality and vividness. With all the splendor of his external triumphs, with all the wealth of his lands and crowns, a profound tragedy and melancholy enshrouded the figure and history of this ruler from his orphaned childhood to his calm and long prepared-for death—a tragedy harmonizing with the black garments worn by the aging Emperor in the Titian portrait, which influenced the later image of him.

The idea of the transitoriness of all earthly things and the inevitability of death remained with Charles throughout his life, and probably helped to keep him from false pride in good times and from despair in bad. The ruler who lived with the high medieval ideal of a universal monarchy, thereby going far beyond the limits of his House's aspirations (which since Rudolf's time had been confined to the scheme of renewing the Hohenstaufen traditions), was no dreamer, romantic, or visionary. His letters and instructions, especially to his son and heir Philip, are suffused with the cool clarity of High Renaissance statesmanship, stressing the subjugation of human passions through reason (*ratio*). The consciousness of his immense responsibility before God for the well-being and spiritual salvation of his subject peoples is the determining element, and from this responsibility arises his duty to conduct all affairs of state most scrupulously. Sober judgment of the strengths and weaknesses of individual servants, counselors, and generals is supplemented by the advice to cultivate an ever-vigilant suspicion of advisors, flatterers, and favorites; this corresponds to his advice to hide one's own feelings and emotions and to let nobody, except God and a confessor, look into one's soul.

It is occasionally chilling to observe the coldbloodedness

with which the probable duration of an old and deserving servant's further usefulness is here estimated (although the successor is always admonished to honor and reward the statesmen and generals grown old in his service), but more than three centuries later other Habsburgs, Field Marshal Archduke Albert or Francis Joseph, display a very similar attitude. Though prominent in the handling of state affairs and in official correspondence, it is not in the least incompatible with the capacity for true human friendship and warmth of heart, demonstrated particularly by Francis Joseph. As we know from many small recorded traits, Charles V, too, was by no means cold and unfeeling. Nor was Charles's son Philip, nor were most of the Habsburgs after Charles V.

Although he went far beyond the framework of Habsburg sovereignty established by Rudolf I, Charles V, in his cool and calculating appraisal of forces at work, and his conscientious, deliberate weighing of the possible consequences of each step, was a true Habsburg and—in the broad sense of the term—also a political realist. His pole star was the high and noble ideal of the imperial office, combined with faith in the divine election of his own House, the "*Maison d'Autriche*." But true to family tradition this most magnificent figure in Habsburg history ended his life in renunciation, resignation, and self-effacement in the consciousness of having done his duty.

10: *Madrid and Vienna*

Charles V has been compared to Columbus, who looked for a shorter route to India but discovered a new world; and also to Luther, who wanted to renew the purity of the old faith but founded a new one. Charles wanted to renew the high medieval ideal of universal monarchy, but in reality he founded the Spanish empire and Spanish hegemony in Europe.

Charles and his son Philip II created the Spanish epoch in Europe, which in the next century was superseded by the French epoch. Philip II is the Louis XIV of the sixteenth century, and his mighty structure, the Escorial, has been called the Spanish Versailles—or better, Versailles is the French Escorial. With Charles's abandonment of the imperial ideal, a period of Spanish predominance (especially in culture and politics) began not only for Europe but also for the House of Habsburg. The period can roughly be supposed to start with either the Religious Peace of Augsburg in 1555, or the Spanish victory over the French at St. Quentin on August 10, 1557 (the feast day of the Spanish saint, Laurence). Between these events lay the abdication of Charles V, the detachment of the Emperor, grown weary of everlasting struggles, from the developments in the empire he could not approve for either political or religious reasons.

The Religious Peace of Augsburg destroyed Habsburg hopes for the establishment of religious unity in Germany, and therewith the possibility—which had reappeared after the defeat of the Schmalkaldic League—of transforming the Empire into a hereditary monarchy and thus setting up a strong central control. Charles's plan for the succession had

foundered on the combined resistance of the younger line of
the House of Habsburg and the German princes; the Peace
of Augsburg was the result of their co-operation. But this
compromise solution in the German sphere of conflict, together with Philip II's accession and the victory at St.
Quentin, meant that henceforth the line ruling Spain became the leaders within the House, while the line of Ferdinand and his successors, though holding the hereditary
German lands and retaining the imperial crown, dwindled
into junior status. The *"Maison d'Autriche"* of Maximilian
and Charles became the *"Casa d'Austria"* of Philip and his
successors.

Though Ferdinand had won a victory over Charles and
Philip in establishing his own and his son's succession in the
Empire, in subsequent periods the Spanish line (not least because of its greater financial and military resources) took
over leadership in the fight against the infidel, the quarrel
with France, the contests with the Papacy, and the global
war between Catholicism and Protestantism. The victory of
Lepanto over the Turkish fleet (1571), decisive for the entire
Mediterranean world, was achieved under the Spanish command of Don John of Austria, the illegitimate son of
Charles V and Barbara Blomberg; the Spanish line carried
on alone the fight against the French Huguenots, the rebellious Netherlanders, and its great and successful seafaring
rival, Elizabethan England.

In Italy, too, as Lords of Milan and Naples, the Spaniards
represented the whole House, and the voice of the Spanish
king—in friendship or enmity—carried more weight with the
Curia than that of the German-Habsburg emperor, power-
less not only in Germany but also in his hereditary Austrian
lands against the advances of the Protestants, and constantly
threatened by the Turkish peril in the east. The age of discovery and overseas conquest, of great naval battles, of the
struggle for control of the sea and for overseas trade, was

naturally an age for seafaring nations, Portuguese, Spaniards, Italians, Dutchmen, English, and French, with whom even the once proud Hanseatic League could not compete. The lands of the German Habsburgs lay outside the sphere of the great decisions; for this one important hour they remained, as it were, in the backyard of history.

When, after Ferdinand I's death in 1564, the lands were divided again among his sons according to the old Habsburg law of inheritance, the eldest, Maximilian, received the imperial crown, the former Albertine lands of Upper and Lower Austria, and also the Bohemian crown lands. Ferdinand founded a new southern Austrian-Tyrolean line, and Charles an inner Austrian-Styrian line, so that a new era seemed to have begun, with the branches divided and inferior in strength to the Diet—whose resistance to the sovereign had been intensified by religious antagonism. Added to this was the constant Turkish threat, which could be only barely restrained by desperate exertions or oppressive payments of tribute. One understands the weakness of the Austrian Habsburgs in the second half of the sixteenth century, and their not very enviable position as poor cousins of the Spanish Habsburgs, who had just reached the height of their power in Europe and the world as a whole. A comparison of the building activity in Spain and Austria at that period—with almost nothing remarkable in the Austrian alpine lands or even in Vienna—indicates which branch of the House was in the ascendant. The protocol of the Emperor's precedence over the Spanish rulers was therefore peculiarly incongruous, and stimulated the unfortunate quarrel between the French and Spanish ambassadors at the Council of Trent in 1562, when the Spaniard (representing the most powerful ruler in Europe) was unwilling to accept third place behind the imperial and French ambassadors. As a result, Philip II requested the Pope to bestow on him the title of *"Emperador de las Indias,"* Emperor of the New World. But the Pope, who

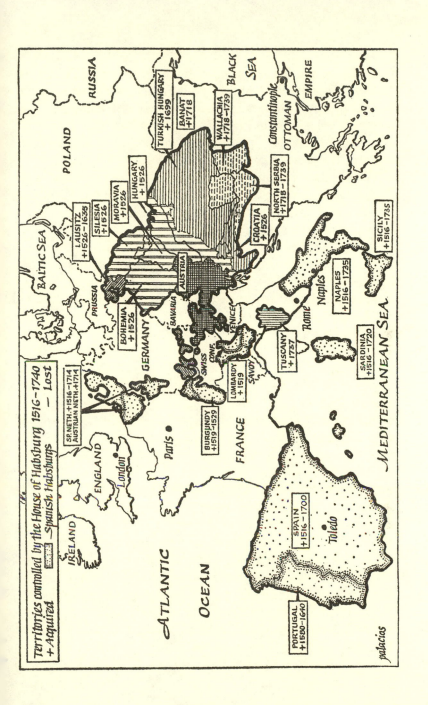

Territories controlled by the House of Habsburg 1516–1740
+ Acquired   — Lost
▓ Spanish Habsburgs

BALTIC SEA

POLAND

RUSSIA

BLACK SEA

OTTOMAN EMPIRE

Constantinople

TURKISH HUNGARY +1699

BANAT +1718

WALLACHIA +1718–1739

MORAVIA +1526

HUNGARY +1526

LAUSITZ +1526–1635

SILESIA +1526

NORTH SERBIA +1718–1739

CROATIA +1526

PRUSSIA

BOHEMIA +1526

AUSTRIA

SICILY +1516–1735

GERMANY

BAVARIA

VENICE

Naples

NAPLES +1516–1735

Rome

SWISS CONF.

SAVOY

LOMBARDY +1519

TUSCANY +1737

SARDINIA +1516–1720

SP. NETH. +1516–1714
AUSTRIAN NETH. +1714

BURGUNDY +1519–1529

FRANCE

MEDITERRANEAN SEA

IRELAND

ENGLAND

London

Paris

ATLANTIC

OCEAN

SPAIN +1516–1700

Toledo

PORTUGAL +1580–1640

palacias

suffered from the Spanish dominance in Italy and the rest of
Europe, did not honor the request.

In 1526, the young King Louis of Hungary and Bohemia
was killed in the battle of Mohács—which was an epoch-
making event from a later historical point of view, that regarded the creation of the Danubian monarchy as the providential and ultimate goal of Habsburg history. But at the
time the inheritance of Hungary brought in, apart from a
not very significant strip of border and a problematical title
and claim, only the continual burden of battles with the
Turks and the Hungarian Magnates. The somewhat safer as-
set of Bohemia was marred by the power of its Diet. After
Ferdinand I's sons had taken over their portions, Maximilian II (whose territory comprised Austria above and below the Enns and the countries that had been subject to
Wenceslas) naturally became most interested in Bohemia,
which was not so exposed to the Turkish danger as were
Vienna and Lower Austria. Maximilian II's son, Emperor
Rudolf II, therefore did not reside in Vienna but in the
Hradčany Palace in Prague, so that the Luxemburg-Albertine
concept was briefly revived.

During the critical situation after the Peace of Augsburg
and the accession of Philip II in Spain, a radical and tempting change of course became possible for the German-Habsburg line, which would have meant the complete disintegration of the dynastic partnership and the rejection of the
Spanish line. Maximilian (who by nature was inclined to Protestantism, hated his Spanish relatives, and also did not get
along with his father, Ferdinand) toyed with the idea of re-
belling against his father with the help of the German Protestant princes, and securing the victory of Lutheranism in
the Empire. If such an alliance between the German Habsburgs and Protestantism had been realized, it would have
fundamentally altered the entire course of Habsburg, German,
and European history. But since the Protestant German

princes were suspicious of Maximilian's suggestion, not wishing to sacrifice their good relations with Emperor Ferdinand to so risky a conspiracy with his son, Maximilian lost confidence in the possibility of a radical change of course with the help of the Lutheran princes and—probably less for religious than for political reasons—again drew closer to Catholicism and finally also to his cousin, brother-in-law, and later son-in-law, Philip II. The danger of an open breach between Vienna and Madrid, which would have become irreparable if they had differed in their religious confessions, was thus averted by the new family connections.

Since Maximilian's double attempt to obtain the Polish crown failed, the Spanish line continued to maintain unchanged its clear and immense superiority over the German line throughout the second half of the sixteenth century and far into the seventeenth. The inevitable loosening of family ties created by the difference in importance and in duties between the two branches was countered by the proven remedy of intermarriage.

It may be difficult for men of our time to understand the mentality that made possible those interfamily ties, so clearly monstrous from the point of view of genetics. It is true that inbreeding had already started earlier, in the intermarriages of the Spanish dynasty with the Portuguese. Behind these marriages between relatives lies the Iberian idea of preserving racial purity, the unsullied blood royal, as contrasted with mixed marriages with the Moors. And probably through the Portuguese dynasty, by way of Joanna the Mad's maternal grandmother, insanity entered the Habsburg bloodline. Maximilian I's mother as well as the mother of Charles the Bold of Burgundy had been Portuguese princesses; the wife of Charles V, Isabella of Portugal, was—through her mother Mary—like her husband a grandchild of the "Catholic Majesties" Ferdinand and Isabella; and Philip II's first marriage (concluded in the early youth of both parties) was also to a

Portuguese princess, the daughter of his mother's brother. With such a degree of inbreeding the pernicious consequences —the intellectual and physical deficiencies of the wretched Don Carlos, child of the first marriage—are not in the least surprising.

The same principle of multiple consanguineous marriages was now applied to the two Habsburg lines. Maximilian II was the husband of the Infanta Mary, a daughter of his uncle Charles V; their daughter, Anne, in 1570 became the fourth wife of Philip II, and bore him—her mother's brother and her father's cousin—the first son capable of ruling, the later King Philip III. One can only be surprised that the negative effects of such inbreeding did not manifest themselves earlier and to an even greater extent. A similar extreme case marked the end of the connection between the two Habsburg lines: Ferdinand III married Mary, the daughter of Philip III and sister of Philip IV; a daughter of this marriage, the Archduchess Mary Anne, was first to have married her uncle's son, Crown Prince Balthasar Carlos, but after his early death she married the widowed Philip IV himself. Leopold I, Ferdinand III's son, in order to strengthen the claims of the Austrian Habsburgs to the Spanish inheritance, married the Infanta Margaret, daughter of his sister Mary Anne and of his uncle Philip IV.

One result of these intermarriages between Madrid and Vienna (to which the Viennese museums and collections owe numerous unique art treasures, among them the series of superb Habsburg portraits by Velásquez) was that the House of Habsburg in the century after Charles V's abdication was regarded by friend and foe alike as basically a unit, in spite of its division into two branches and the tensions unavoidable within the family. In fact, the balance between the attempts to preserve family unity and the divisive tendencies (which inevitably and repeatedly resulted from the highly divergent interests of the subject countries and the rivalry of the two courts) provides the main theme of Habsburg family history in this century.

It was important, therefore, that the head of the Spanish line, Charles V's son and heir, King Philip II, ruled for more than four decades (1556–98), almost the entire second half of the century; after the death of Emperor Ferdinand I in 1564, and all the more after his son, Maximilian II, died in 1576, Philip, as the most significant and powerful European prince, was regarded as the head of the entire House and its undisputed authority. The style of life and government developed by Charles V and extended by Philip II became an obligatory mold for the whole House. Of course not all later Habsburgs patterned their lives and governments according to the high principles and demands of Charles and Philip —indeed Philip's son and grandson no longer did so—but this style amalgamated the individual family traditions and continued to affect the best rulers as an inspiring and controlling system of values, something much stronger than a mere biological relationship. Even the more mediocre and weak characters were not left entirely untouched.

The acutely observant Venetian ambassadors to the imperial court reported most vividly on the difference in style of government between the two Habsburg lines, and how, through the education of Maximilian's sons at the court of Philip II, the "Spanish" example became binding also on the German Habsburgs. In 1574, Giovanni Corraro contrasted the agreeable, charming, cordial, quick, and linguistically gifted Maximilian II (who mastered Czech and Hungarian as well as Latin, German, Italian, French, and Spanish), with his sons Rudolf and Ernest, who had just returned from Spain:

> So these princes also have retained from their Spanish education something that can be just as harmful to them as the other[1] can

[1] The strictly Catholic frame of mind.

be useful, to wit, a certain hauteur, be it in walking, be it in every
other bodily movement, which makes them—I do not wish to say
hated, in order to avoid the unpleasant word—but in any case less
popular than they could be. For this in every respect runs counter
to the local custom here, which demands of the sovereign a certain
familiar manner of speech, and is regarded as an attribute imported
from Spain, which is certainly considered bad and detestable; and
when they had come from Spain, His Majesty[2] noted this and
drew their attention to it and ordered them to change their behavior
(*che mutassero stile*). And he did this several times, as is known,
and since it did not help, or only very little, one day he had to say
laughingly—in order to save their reputation—that they also be-
haved that way with him. And in this he wanted to explain that
they did not do it out of conceit, but because it was a deeply
rooted habit that they could hardly change. And certainly they
are known by those who serve them or who have closer contact
with them as very polite princes with good gifts; but the multitude,
which cannot see that far and depends on external appearance,
takes offense and interprets it as conceit, and this all the more because they are not very talkative by nature. But what harms their
credit most is the comparison with their father, who is so affable
and polite with everybody, and hardly anybody, or better nobody,
no matter how quick or well brought up, is able to make use of
words, looks, or gestures as he can, and nobody has by nature such
a pleasant expression, which completely captures the affection of all
who see him, as does His Majesty; and even the poorest little old
woman can, as he comes from mass or goes anywhere at all, stop
him and freely open her heart to him.

North of the Alps, too, the friendly Maximilian I and the
much more reserved Charles V, or later the popular Ferdinand I and the unpopular Infante Philip II, were similarly
compared. The type of sovereign represented by Charles V
and his son remained the model for the German Habsburg
line from Maximilian II's sons, who were educated at Philip
II's court, down to Leopold I and Charles VI. In the report
by the Venetian ambassador, *stile* is used for the frigid
demeanor of the princes, and the style of sovereignty taken

[2] Maximilian II.

over by the German from the more powerful Spanish Habsburg line was indeed different. Only after the Spanish line had become extinct did the Vienna line develop a new style that was again reminiscent of Maximilian II's (traces of it appeared first with Joseph I, and later it matured with Maria Theresa and Joseph II), although in subsequent periods, under the emperors Francis or Francis Joseph, vestiges of the style developed by Philip II still lingered. These traits were very clearly recognized by the enemies of the House, and the attacks on Francis Joseph, under the character of Philip (in the period of the Italian Risorgimento, for instance in Verdi's *Don Carlos*), contained a kernel of historic truth in spite of their malicious exaggeration.

Philip II was painted in the blackest colors by hostile historians and men of letters during the centuries of Enlightenment and liberalism, and only recently has a change in opinion begun to make itself felt. Probably it was unavoidable that, in the effort to do Philip justice, there has been some error and exaggeration on the other side.

Philip was no genius, reformer, or innovator; as a matter of principle he did not embark on new ventures. Stamped for life by parental authority, he held tenaciously to the advice and teaching repeatedly showered upon him in innumerable letters, memoranda, and political testaments by his much beloved and revered father. Awareness of his responsibility for the nation entrusted to him through God's grace, his duty to "enable it to live in peace and quiet, in justice and order," and belief that he would have to give account of his stewardship to God, were the principal guides of his life and government (as Erasmus had laid them down in his ideal image of the Christian prince). Thus his character achieved in imposing integration. Responsibility and duty, thorough deliberation and conscientious reflection before each decision (which sometimes bordered on vacillation), painstaking execution of affairs of state and bureaucratically exact management of files were the fruits of his father's teaching, and they suited both family traditions and his inherited traits of character.

The idea of universality, which had played such an important role for the father, gave place for the son (who had no imperial crown) to the importance of the Spanish hegemony, because he believed that the "Catholic Majesty" of Spain was appointed to lead Christendom, and that God had entrusted him with the preservation of true religion and faith, and the defense of Christ's people against external and internal enemies, unbelievers and heretics. Closely associated with the idea of preserving the purity of religion was the Iberian ideal of preserving racial purity, the opposition to any admixture of Moorish or Jewish blood, and so there arose a belief in the particular destiny of the royal bloodline and in the exaltation and special consecration of the royal House and the sacred person of the monarch above all other mortals.

The segregation of the ruling dynasty from the rest of the world, and of the consecrated person of the monarch even from the court circle, was achieved by the further development and intensification of court ceremonial. This was paralleled by the new importance of Madrid, which hitherto had been an insignificant town outside the main stream of national life, trade, and traffic, as the capital; and by the basic design for the Escorial and the choice of its site and architecture. In *Words and Deeds of the King Don Philip II* a contemporary, Baltasar Porreño, has vividly and very graphically described the existence of this inviolable zone around the royal person, "A certain line of demarcation existed that could not be crossed by even the most intimate because, as soon as he reached it, he fell on his face."

The creation of this inviolable zone fitted Charles V's admonition to his son that, even with his closest advisors, he should try to hide his feelings, and probably also suited

Philip's basically shy, repressed, and introverted nature; at the same time it established a reverential awe of the ruler and strengthened his authority over his entourage as well as over the people as a whole. Philip repeatedly restrained his successful military leaders when they wished to exploit a victory by destroying the enemy—most notably in the case of his half brother, the naval hero Don John of Austria, after Lepanto.

Various explanations for this phenomenon have been attempted: anxious hesitation and irresoluteness, envy of the generals' popularity by a ruler who knew that he lacked military gifts, or worry that his generals might "grow above his head" and break through the invisible, inviolable zone. Probably all these reasons entered in, as well as the metaphysical fear that God might punish the arrogance of the victor through a new defeat, and the reluctance to assume the weight of responsibility, the unwillingness—deeply rooted in Habsburg family tradition—to entrust the fate of the House to the hazards of war any more frequently than necessary. Conversely, he did not withdraw his favor from a beaten military leader, like the Duke of Medina-Sidonia, leader of the great Armada against Elizabethan England; it is uncertain whether the King actually spoke the words put into his mouth by Schiller in his *Don Carlos*, that he had sent the admiral out against human, not natural, forces.

Disimular, the dissembling of one's feelings, which Charles so insistently recommended to his son, was cultivated by Philip to such a degree that he hid them not only from his contemporaries but also from posterity; for a long time Philip was thought to have been altogether incapable of emotion—he had not just hidden his feelings but had never had any. Only the discovery of letters to his daughters destroyed this notion, which was also contradicted by the sincere affection that his wives felt for him, although, of the King's four marriages, at most the first had been partly arranged for love, while the other three had been exclusively political matches made to safeguard the continuation of the dynasty.

It is true that a somber shadow lay over the king's domestic life, the tragedy of the Crown Prince Don Carlos, the wretched victim of Iberian inbreeding. King Philip's concealment of his grief and his proud rebuffs to the world's curiosity about his mentally and physically deformed child, during Don Carlos's lifetime and after his death in his father's care, are reminiscent of the behavior of a later Habsburg, Emperor Francis Joseph, after the tragic death of the Crown Prince at Mayerling. By their proud silence and secrecy both rulers only encouraged the growth of fantastic legends; both were unjustly accused of coldness, bureaucratic dryness, and heartlessness, by contemporaries and posterity, while in fact the consciousness of a higher responsibility triumphed over their real paternal feelings. Neither Philip II nor Francis Joseph I lacked the Habsburg family affection that is encountered in all centuries (though, not surprisingly, it is more clearly evident in those members of the House not burdened with sovereignty); the gentleness and tenderness of the relations between husbands and wives, parents and children, and brothers and sisters is amply documented.

The tremendous memorial to Philip II's noble conception of his sovereign office and of the honor of his family became the Escorial, near Madrid, dedicated to St. Laurence, the Spanish martyr on whose feast day the victory of St. Quentin had been won. Maximilian's idea of his Innsbruck tomb as a place of prayer for the souls of all the deceased members and ancestors of the House was expanded in the Escorial (following a recommendation in Charles V's will) into a combination of palace and burial place, a union of the dead and living members of the House. Combined with this was the purely religious dedication of the building, whose cornerstone was laid in the same month and year as the conclusion of the Council of Trent.

The Escorial has properly been called the King's "Monumental Credo" (Georg Weise), a commemoration of his efforts to keep the faith and his race free from taint. As a research institute and model farm, as an autarchic community directed by monks (who undertook all forms of agriculture, including the growing of fruit, vegetables, and flowers), and as the "source and fountain of all sciences," the Escorial was to be a *summa* of human faith, thought, and work—the most perfect incarnation of the old European idea of the House— as well as a symbol, in its simple yet magnificent architecture, of "majesty and grandeur, authority and aristocracy, dignity and nobility."

In political questions Philip, the champion of Catholicism in the religious-political conflict convulsing all of Europe, and the opponent of Elizabethan England, the French Huguenots, and the German and Dutch Protestants, assumed his father's independent attitude to the Roman Curia. The Jesuits, vowed to unconditional obedience to the Pope, played no significant role at his court, and in the following century the two Habsburg lines still differed in their treatment of the society. In Vienna the Jesuits determined the entire political, religious, and cultural life, as confessors, royal tutors, university professors, and preachers, whereas they were not welcome at the court of Madrid.

It may seem paradoxical that Ferdinand I (who, though personally a strict Catholic, was inclined to make compromises with and concessions to the Protestants), even before the ratification of the Peace of Augsburg, called the first German Jesuits, under Peter Canisius, to Vienna. There, as well as at the court of the art-loving Archduke Ferdinand in Innsbruck, Canisius established the first centers of the Counter Reformation in the alpine regions. Nevertheless, under Ferdinand I and of course all the more under his son

Maximilian II, who was inclined toward Protestantism, the number of adherents to the new faith in the German Habsburg lands steadily increased. Maximilian's oldest son, Emperor Rudolf II, could not decisively counter the power of the Protestant Estates. He had been educated in Spain and his religion was entirely fashioned after the great model of Philip II; he was a ruler sympathetic to the arts and sciences, but politically incompetent and even more pathologically indecisive than his ancestor Frederick III. However, his younger brother, Archduke Ernest, who had been educated in the same religious spirit but was much more forceful than Rudolf, began a revival of Catholicism when he was governor of Upper and Lower Austria. The House of Habsburg also acquired an impressive statesman in Melchior Khlesl, who began life as the son of a Viennese Lutheran master baker, and ended it as a cardinal.

In fact, in the first fifteen years of the new century, the "Brothers' Quarrel" between the politically timorous Rudolf (who devoted himself in his Prague castle entirely to alchemy, astrology, and art collecting), and the other members of the House, led by his brother Matthias, only further strengthened the power of the Protestant Estates. As in the late medieval period of conflict between the princes of the separate branches, or the brothers' quarrel between Frederick III and Albert VI, it was the territorial Diets who profited most from a situation that seemed doubly dangerous because Austria's Protestant nobility had finally found in Georg Erasmus von Tschernembl the energetic leader whom it had lacked so long. Faced by the Protestant threat, the Turkish danger, the struggle with the Upper Hungarian and Transylvanian magnates, and the impending storm of religious-political battle in the Empire, Ferdinand I's descendants really were able to do hardly anything except—as one of the characters in Grillparzer's *Bruderzwist* (*Brothers' Quarrel*) laments—"*Auf halben Wegen und zu halber Tat mit halben Mitteln zauderhaft zu streben"* ("Strive tremulously with half the means halfway to half a deed").

As in the fifteenth century, the Styrian-Central Austrian line was destined to bring the House out of the doldrums again. In 1579, three years after the death of Maximilian II, his younger brother, Archduke Charles, reached a secret agreement in Munich with his father-in-law, the Duke of Bavaria, to revive Catholicism in the Austrian alpine regions. Thus the decisive impulses for the Austrian Counter Reformation emanated not from Spain but from Bavaria. Ferdinand II, Archduke Charles's son and a former student at the Jesuit school in Ingolstadt, began to put the Counter Reformation into force, after his father had already begun it in Styria. Ferdinand started first with his inherited domains and then, becoming heir to the Emperor Matthias who had died without issue in 1619, he enforced it with severity in Bohemia and Upper and Lower Austria; finally, with the Edict of Restitution of 1629, he tried to do the same in the Empire.

Before succeeding his cousin Matthias, Ferdinand had already charted the future course of his government in two political actions. The first was a settlement with the Spanish line. Philip III, son of Philip II and Archduchess Anne, had entered a claim to Austria and Styria, the vacant patrimony of the oldest German Habsburg line,[3] because he was a grandson of Maximilian II, and disputed the rights of Ferdinand and his descendants since Ferdinand was only Maximilian's nephew. An agreement was reached after extended negotiations between the brothers-in-law (for Philip III had married Ferdinand's sister Margaret). In the secret treaty named for Oñate, the Spanish ambassador who concluded it with Ferdinand in 1617 at Prague, Philip renounced his claims and Ferdinand in turn promised the Spaniards Alsace, important for the passage of Spanish troops from Italy to the Netherlands.

[3] Maximilian II's sons had died without issue.

As a matter of fact, Ferdinand never did surrender Alsace; Philip's further claims were satisfied by the transfer of some imperial fiefs in northern Italy. The Oñate treaty was historically significant because it re-established friendly relations between the two lines; without Spanish wealth Ferdinand could not have waged the great war impending in Germany. The second measure was the ousting of Emperor Matthias's chief counselor, Cardinal Khlesl, who was hostile to the close alliance between Ferdinand and the Spaniards and who, contrary to his first violent hatred of the Protestants, now favored a compromise between the confessions in the Habsburg patrimonies as well as in the Empire. On Ferdinand's order Khlesl was arrested on July 20, 1618, in the *Hofburg*.

Two months earlier, on May 23, imperial counselors had been literally thrown out by Bohemian Protestant nobles in the Defenestration of Prague. The great war began: in Germany between the two religious and political camps; in Austria with an additional struggle between the sovereign and the Diets; in the Empire between the Emperor and the imperial Diet; and in the whole of Europe between the united lines of the House of Habsburg and the allied monarchies of France and Sweden.

In the Battle of the White Mountain, the first great and decisive engagement of the Thirty Years' War, fought near Prague on November 8, 1620, Ferdinand II (who had in the meantime been elected Emperor) vanquished the Bohemian rebels and their "Winter King," Frederick of the Palatinate, with the help of Bavarian arms and Spanish money. Lutheran Saxony took the Catholic Emperor's side against the Calvinist from the Palatinate. In Rome the great event was celebrated with the building of Santa Maria della Vittoria. The victory of the Catholic Counter Reformation and of absolute monarchy in the Austrian dominions had been decided. But Ferdinand's attempt to repeat the same triumphs in the empire failed because of the intervention of foreign powers, espe-

cially Sweden and France. Even the victory at Nördlingen
on September 6,1634, achieved by the co-operation of imperial troops under the command of the "King of Hungary"
(later Emperor Ferdinand III), and Spanish troops com-
manded by the Cardinal Infante Ferdinand (Philip IV's
brother), could not redress the balance. The prospect of a
general peace promised by the treaty between the Emperor
and the Lutheran-North German Diets, concluded in
Prague in 1635, proved deceptive. Battles and negotiations
continued for another decade and, during it, the alliance between the two Habsburg lines was shattered.

Spanish Habsburg power had been declining ever since the
end of the "great Armada" and even more noticeably after
the death of Philip II. His son, Philip III, and his grandson,
Philip IV, were weak, insignificant rulers, genetically much
enfeebled after the numerous preceding intermarriages, who
turned over the governmental authority to their favorites
(*Privados*)—Philip III to the Duke of Lerma, and Philip IV
to the Count of Olivares, Duke of Santander. Under these
favorites the pendulum swung from religious to political
struggles, following the trend of the times and the developments in neighboring France. When the French religious
civil war, in which Philip had intervened on the Catholic side,
had ended, and the French monarchy had gained new
strength, the old quarrel broke out again between France and
Spain.

At the beginning and end of the war of religion Madrid
and Vienna were out of step with each other in their pursuit
of major aims, a discrepancy characteristic of the "west-east
cultural gradient," or the time it took for Spanish ideas to
take root in Austria. When Philip II, as the leader of a European Catholicism revivified by the Council of Trent, had
long been engaged in a struggle with Calvinism that embraced
all of western and southern Europe, the German Habsburgs
still hoped to maintain peace in Germany and their own

dominions by an amicable settlement with the Lutherans, and to heal the schism peacefully. With the accession of Philip IV in 1621, and the renewed outbreak of the war with France in 1622, the makers of Spanish policy thought chiefly of their struggle for power with France, while Germany at the same time was experiencing the horrors of a civil war that was, at least initially, religious.

Contrary to the conventional idea, shaped by literary tradition, of Spanish zeal in the Counter Reformation, the negotiations between Madrid and Vienna that continued throughout the Thirty Years' War reveal repeatedly that the Spaniards were not bigoted, but more ready than the Austrians to make concessions to the Protestants. Even the Spanish Capuchin Quiroga, who had come to the Viennese court as confessor to a Spanish Infanta, and who was a bitter enemy of the Jesuits then setting the tone in Vienna, emphatically advocated peace with the German Lutherans. The Spaniards defended Wallenstein as long as possible, for they saw in him the champion of peace in the Empire (if concessions were made by both sides and the imperial authority, as opposed to the power of the princes, were enforced—a program that entirely fitted their own political concepts).

The Spaniards were principally interested in seeing that the Emperor, by making peace with the German Protestants, Denmark, and Sweden, could free sufficient forces to help them in their fight against France. They therefore complained that the Viennese court, which was always asking for and receiving money, used it not to raise troops for the western theater of operations against France, but either for the war against Sweden or for the maintenance of the imperial household. Naturally Ferdinand II and his son, Ferdinand III, felt the Swedes to be a more immediate danger than the relatively remote French. Ferdinand's intransigent hostility to the south German Protestants, whose "exclusion" from the Treaty of Prague contributed essentially to its failure, and his stubborn determination to reconvert at least southern Germany, were partly motivated by his hope of confiscating the "rebels'" property in order to replenish his perpetually depleted coffers.

Finally, when the length of the war and the decline of the Spanish economy and finances cut down the subsidies to a trickle, Madrid's and Vienna's political interests diverged more and more openly. In the negotiations leading to the Peace of Westphalia Ferdinand III, though apparently following the Spaniards' political lesson, in fact detached himself completely from Madrid. He made an independent peace with Sweden and France on behalf of the Empire and his own dominions, leaving his brother-in-law Philip IV—who also became his son-in-law—to continue the war against France alone. Ferdinand's ambassador in Madrid, General Francesco Carretto, Marquis of Grana, was instructed to persuade Philip IV that an unavoidable emergency had compelled the Emperor to conclude the peace. In spite of everything, the relationship between the two Habsburg lines was still so close that Philip agreed to this fiction of duress.

In the following spring Ferdinand's daughter, Mary Anne, married the widowed Philip IV. However, the Emperor's proposal of a match between his son and heir, Archduke Ferdinand, and Philip's older daughter, Maria Theresa, was energetically turned down by Madrid. The prince, who had already traveled with his sister to Rovereto (on the border between the German and Spanish Habsburg lands), was told that he would not be received in Spain. The Spanish princess's hand was later given to Louis XIV, himself the son of a Spanish Habsburg mother (sister to Philip IV, who was therefore both uncle and father-in-law of the Sun King); his claims to the Spanish inheritance were derived from this marriage.

The era of Habsburg world power, the sixteenth and seventeenth centuries, was also the high point for Habsburg patronage and industrious collecting of the arts, probably stimulated because the Spanish and Austrian lines profitably vied with each other throughout Europe. Earlier Habsburgs had eagerly acquired jewels, works of art, and magnificent books (in this respect Frederick III and Maximilian I had been not only true Renaissance princess in their love of splendor, but also knowledgeable and understanding patrons).

A surprising number of Ferdinand I's sons and grandsons were deeply interested in art, and were possessed by a singular passion for collecting that has hardly ever been matched in history. They created a new type of private gallery (*Kunstkammer*). Maximilian II, connoisseur and collector of pictures, and his brothers, Archduke Ferdinand of Tyrol (founder of the world-famous Ambras collection), and Charles (who tried to compete with his brothers in Graz), but particularly Rudolf II, the greatest imperial lover of the arts, and his brothers Ernest, Maximilian *"the Deutschmeister"* (Grand Master of the Teutonic Order for the German territories), and Albert VII, Regent of the Netherlands, all distinguished themselves as much through their generosity as through the sure touch and universality of their connoisseurship. It embraced works ancient, medieval, and contemporary, by Italian, Spanish, German, and Dutch artists, created in extremely different styles and epochs, and took in the widest assortment of art forms, from painting to armor, and from sculpture to the making of musical instruments.

The connection with the Netherlands, where members of the German Habsburg line (like Archduke Albert, Rudolf II's brother, and later Archduke Leopold William, Emperor Ferdinand III's brother) were active both as regents and art collectors, proved particularly fruitful. Certainly the sovereigns in particular, but also their younger brothers and sisters and collateral relatives, were influenced by the political idea of heightening the magnificence of their House, yet they were distinguished also by a genuine and discriminating connoisseurship, whose wide horizon corresponded to the grandly conceived political theories of the *Casa d'Austria*.

11: The Rulers during the Austrian Baroque Period

The Thirty Years' War brought religious and political victory to the Habsburg dynasty in its own original territory. But in the empire Ferdinand II's attempt to enforce his claim to sovereignty had been wrecked by the opposition of foreign powers and the imperial princes, including the Catholic ones. So it was settled that the Habsburgs could indeed establish an absolute monarchy—which now became the pattern in Central and eastern Europe as well—in their original domain, but not in the empire. Certainly their position in their own lands received additional glory because they kept the venerable and honored imperial crown, but their tenuous connection with the almost extinct Madrid branch (which was still preserved, if only in hope of the Spanish inheritance) and their religious and traditional sense of responsibility, hindered them from developing an unfettered absolutism. As a result, quite apart from their tendency to conserve rather than to make innovations, the Habsburgs almost inevitably lagged somewhat behind in the general development of absolutist power that was taking place in the other European states. The peculiar character of the group of German Habsburg possessions, as well as the strongly developed and conscious individuality of the separate lands, where the power of the Diets had not yet been completely broken but only restricted, favored the tendency to continue as long as possible the old political forms and traditions.

After the Battle of the White Mountain, Ferdinand II decreed in his will, made in 1621, that the German Habsburg lands were not to be partitioned in the future; but only four years later he was forced to cede the Tyrol, the lands north of the Alps, and Alsace, to his brother Leopold, though according to the Oñate treaty Alsace had really been assigned to the Spanish crown. This group of countries did not revert to the entire House until 1665, when, shortly before the extinction of the Spanish line, the last division of the family into branches ended.

Similar hesitations and delays attended the establishment in the Habsburg domains of the secular theory of the primacy of the state, detached entirely from its religious foundation. Only "unavoidably necessary" steps were taken, like the proceedings against Wallenstein, or the Peace of Prague and the Treaty of Westphalia, and these were always followed by periods of stagnation or even regression. Almost no decisive, creative, or inventive act took place before the old-Hapsburg male line ended.

Nevertheless the period after the Battle of the White Mountain saw a new surge of Habsburg power. The victory of the Counter Reformation was a triumph for the ruling dynasty, and vice versa. Salvation at the eleventh hour, symbolized by the story of Emperor Ferdinand II's rescue when Dampierre's cuirassiers broke through the rebel Protestant forces besieging the *Hofburg,* was seen as fresh proof of the dynasty's special election. The property confiscations, executions, and expulsions of the rebel aristocracy and those Protestants who refused to yield to pressure, created an opportunity for the ruler's own newly created aristocracy (Walloon, Spanish, Italian, and French) to acquire for nothing vacant lands and titles in Bohemia and Austria. These gentry, no longer so closely bound to their domains as the old landed families had been, did not cause so many political difficulties and remained loyal to the dynasty that had created or ennobled them. In earlier times the Habsburgs had repeatedly imported servants and counselors from their western possessions into Austria, and through gifts, infeudations, and intermarriages had incorporated them into the native aristocracy;

the incursion of Ferdinand I's Spanish counselors, typified by the much detested soldier of fortune, Salamanca, had been particularly strong. Now, in the course of the Counter Reformation, the character and composition of the Austrian nobility were radically changed, and the new aristocracy, often consisting of the families of generals who had been in the Thirty Years' War, or later in the Turkish and French Wars, made up the court society and choir of pomp below the apotheosis of the dynasty.

The tendency of the period to set the monarch on a pedestal and regard him as a hero or even a god, and the Baroque delight in grand ceremonial gestures, laurel wreaths, flowing draperies, and fanfares of trumpets, coincided with the newly increased power of the *Domus Austriae*. The simultaneous triumph of the Counter Reformation meant that everywhere cults of rulers and saints, and the glorification of the House of Habsburg as well as of the victorious Catholic Church, intermingled. The welcoming imperial double eagle and the coats of arms of Habsburg lands that appeared on the Baroque façades superimposed on old Gothic churches, and the pillars of the Holy Trinity or of Mary that shot up in the markets and city squares of the Bohemian-Austrian territories, were triumphal emblems for the Catholic Church and also for the ruling dynasty; the great pilgrimages and processions—like the Corpus Christi procession, in which, from the time of Ferdinand II, the Emperor himself and the members of the imperial family expressed the special Habsburg veneration for the Eucharist by walking behind the Holy of Holies—were festive parades of the dynasty as well as the Church. The cult of regional patron saints, St. Leopold the Markgrave in Lower Austria, St. Florian in Upper Austria, St. Notburga in the Tyrol, and St. John Nepomuk in Bohemia, underlined the close connection between religion and politics. John Nepomuk, martyr to the secrecy of the confessional, who was thrown from a bridge into the Moldau because he refused to reveal to the Bohemian King Wenceslas IV the confession of his wife, Queen Joan, became one of the favorite saints of the Austrian Baroque. His statue was not only set up on bridges throughout the country (because, for obvious reasons, he was a patron saint of bridges), it frequently adorned churches built or remodeled in that period. As confessor to a queen he symbolized the union between ecclesiastical and temporal power, and was a clerical counterpart to the canonized ruler, Markgrave Leopold. The joint appearance of the Austrian and the Bohemian saints also suggested the union of the two countries. In the imperial House itself the cult of the Habsburg family saints was much fostered, and stimulated the last flowering of the Pierleoni theory of the family's descent (because it established especially the dynasty's connection with popes and saints).

In subsequent ages it became significant for the Church in Austria that it overcame the Reformation crisis not by its own strength but only with political help, the sword of the Habsburgs. The Church's dependence on, and subjugation to, the ruling House entailed advantages and privileges, but also disadvantages and restrictions of freedom; for Austrian Catholicism the Habsburg scepter was both a prop and a scourge.

Ferdinand II's attitude to the Church was that of a humble son and a strict master. Though lacking in importance as a man and as a politician, and able to make up his mind only after long deliberation and doubt, he took very seriously indeed his responsibility to God and the Church, as he had learned to see it during his education by the Ingolstadt Jesuits. Before every important decision he asked his confessors and theologians if the intended step were in some way detrimental to religion, and, to relieve his conscience, before especially weighty decisions he convened regular theological assemblies which, naturally enough (and particularly when they dealt with political and military questions and had to choose between peace or war) could not always reach unanimity. On really crucial political issues, therefore, the opinion of the political counselors usually proved decisive. At the same time, though Ferdinand completely shared the idea of his time that political union must also mean religious union, he subjected the Church in his domains to strict supervision, made the holding of episcopal visitations dependent on governmental approval, forbade the bishops to publish papal decretals and, if political interests demanded, disregarded ecclesiastical law; in this respect his son and successor, Ferdinand III, who brought the Peace of Westphalia to a fortunate conclusion in the face of papal protests, was probably even more stubborn. With some justification, therefore, the two Ferdinands have been called forerunners of *Josephinismus*, as applied not to philosophical enlightenment, but to canon law.

Habsburg piety in the age of the Baroque and the Counter Reformation thus reveals strange political traits, almost those of a state church, which hardly fit into our modern categories, founded as they are on the conscious or unconscious assumption of a separation in principle between religion and politics. Even the concept of a particular Habsburg piety, the *Pietas Austriaca*, may appear odd to us. If found expression in certain forms of worship and objects of devotion that, in line with contemporary ideas, had always been specially cultivated by the House of Habsburg. In all of them Habsburg history and legend merged with the religious inclinations of the Counter Reformation, and ecclesiastical and political symbols of sovereignty were mixed.

The veneration of the Eucharist was closely linked, through the legend of Rudolf of Habsburg's encounter with the priest, to the belief in the House's divine vocation to sovereignty. Because Rudolf the Ancestor had shown such reverence to the Eucharist, he and his descendants had been wonderfully raised above their fellows. At the same time, this veneration had a topical religious and political significance in the fight against Protestantism, for the confessants could be distinguished by the way in which they received communion, and the Catholic form of communicating was regarded as a sign of reconversion for all those who had been brought back to the fold by force of persuasion. The pilgrimages to places where there were miraculous Hosts, the encouragement of frequent communion by the imperial family at court, and by its subjects, the particularly solemn and ceremonious celebration of the Feast of Corpus Christi by the Emperor and his family, and finally innumerable representations in art of the glorification of the Sacrament, were all significant politically and dynastically as well as ecclesiastically.

The same was true of the veneration of the Virgin Mary; the dynasty and the whole country were placed under the special protection of the Queen of Heaven, the *Magna Mater Austriae*, whose most important shrine, Mariazell, became "a sort of Austrian state sanctuary" (Borodajkewycz). The crown used in pictures and statues of the coronation of the Virgin, a popular subject at that time, was copied from the Habsburg crown made at the time of Rudolf II—the crown of the later "Austrian Empire"—again showing the intermingling of ecclesiastical and dynastic ideas. This was particularly apparent when the Virgin was represented as being crowned by the Trinity, because God's dominion over the world also suggested the Emperor's sovereignty.

The cross in the *Pietas crucis* also symbolized not only religious but political sovereignty and victory, for the cross was raised as a sign of victory over unbelievers and heretics, it commemorated the vision of the first Christian Emperor, Constantine (*in hoc signo vinces*), and it brought to mind the legend of Rudolf the Ancestor and the crucifix as the House's scepter. The imperial quarters in Austrian religious foundations demonstrated how, as in the great Spanish model of the Escorial, ecclesiastical and temporal architectural styles merged to glorify the dynasty and its faith.

Side by side with the *Pietas Austriaca* appeared the *Clementia Austriaca,* the "inherited disposition to mercy, benevolence, [and] leniency," the "native Austrian mildness and clemency," which down the centuries is invoked in almost identical phrases in Habsburg orders, edicts, letters, and other official documents. In Ferdinand II's mouth the formula may seem cruelly ironic (especially in connection with the harsh punitive and vindictive measures taken in Bohemia after 1620). However, an epoch like ours, which has witnessed and still witnesses many worse atrocities, may perhaps judge more leniently the penal code that, after a bloody civil war, restricted the death penalty (though administered in the barbaric forms of the period) to the small group of ringleaders, while simply confiscating the property of most of the rebellious nobles. Real blood baths are rare in Habsburg history, perhaps because of the family's religious principles, disinclination for sweeping measures, desire for compromise and peace, or even its always precarious and dangerous position during the early centuries of the modern period. The formula of "Austrian clemency," once coined, showed rulers of later generations where their duty lay. As an integral part of the Habsburg tradition of administration, it was accepted as a matter of course by subjects and enemies alike. The result was that, when Habsburg rulers were driven by extreme danger to severe measures of repression or revenge, they were repoached far more than were the harsher rulers of other countries, because they seemed to have broken a binding rule of the game.

The Baroque Age, which for Austria's intellectual and cultural history lies between the Battle of the White Mountain and the accession of Maria Theresa (1620 and 1740), became the heroic period for the German House of Habsburg. In power politics the ascending Viennese line took over from the declining Madrid line the principal burden of the fight against the infidels in the east and the French in the west; both the Counter Reformation and the dynasty were triumphant. The relief of Vienna and the victory over the army of Kara Mustafa (1683) represented the great military and political turning point, which was marked dynastically by the accession of Leopold I in 1658. If one continues to call the whole period Baroque—although "the Age of the Habsburgs" has been suggested as appropriate—the term must be understood to apply not merely to the arts but to a general intellectual, religious, political, and economic style. The reigns of the two Ferdinands from 1620 to 1657 formed Austrian Early Baroque, the reign of Leopold I (1657 to 1705) High Baroque, and those of his two sons, Joseph I and Charles VI (1705 to 1740), Late Baroque.

Leopold I was destined and educated for the Church, and became heir to the throne only after his elder brother Ferdinand's early death. With a German Habsburg father and a Spanish Habsburg mother (the Infanta Mary Anne), he had all the Habsburg physical attributes in an extreme form—the long narrow face, the large (and in all portraits somewhat tired-looking) eyes, the long, slightly hooked nose, and, above all, the "Habsburg lip"—a protruding lower lip—and the long, jutting, pointed chin. Many portraits of the Emperor look like involuntary caricatures, and only a few, like the wonderful red chalk drawing by Joachim Sandrart, convey an idea of the dignity and majesty that he evidently possessed.

Like Philip II, whom he resembled in several ways, he was no political or military genius, and abstained from military ventures, as did the Habsburgs generally throughout almost three centuries, from Maximilian I to Archduke Charles (the victor of Aspern), because they never displayed any marked gifts as military leaders. Leopold I's contemporaries taxed him with indecision, and later historians were even more emphatic about it. His behavior to the Hungarian Protestants showed the limitations imposed on his political insight by his religious intolerance, and he contributed decisively to the involvement of his House in an exhausting war on two fronts, so that it did not have its hands free for the great struggle for the Spanish inheritance. But Leopold must be credited with great political acumen for having recognized so early the genius of Prince Eugene of Savory, and having stood by him in spite of all the enemies he had at court. Like many other Habsburgs, Leopold achieved more by leaving things alone, by not being obstructive, by careful deliberation before fateful decisions, and by maintaining his own inner balance in the face of misfortunes and reverses, than by bold deeds or innovations. His religious commitments and probably also his inborn character prevented him from succumbing, in that period of ebullient and unrestrained royal absolutism, to the temptation of self-deification, so that he survives not as "Leopold the Great," as the Baroque court historians called him, but as a ruler hard-pressed by Turks in the east and French in the west. On the memorial pillar near the Viennese city moat (*Graben*), he is represented as both exalted and humble, offering thanksgiving to God for the deliverance of his city from the plague.

Leopold's first wife was his Spanish cousin Margaret, a daughter of Philip IV: the second was Claudia Felicitas, an Austrian archduchess; the third, a German princess, Eleanor of Pfalz-Neuburg, was the mother of his two sons Joseph and Charles (later Emperors), who in their turn also married German princesses. This indicates a change that was further promoted by the quarrel with the Bourbons and the extinction of the Spanish Habsburg line. German national consciousness and imperial patriotism had grown so strong and had proved politically so powerful in the second half of the Thirty Years' War that even the state chancelleries had to take them into account; now nationalism flared up still more

violently in reaction to the claims of Louis XIV. The imperial court of Vienna responded, and Leopold tried to create a
united German front against France by making concessions
to the more important German princes, granting a ninth
Electoral title to Hanover, and recognizing Prussia as a monarchy. He also engaged Hans Jakob Wagner von Wagenfels,
the author of *Ehren-Ruff Teutschlands, der Teutschen und
ihres Reiches* (*A Call to the Honor of Germany, the Germans, and their Empire*) as tutor in history (*Intructor in
historicis et politicis*) to his thirteen-year-old son, later the
Emperor Joseph I.

The old problem of the tension between eastern and
western commitments took a new form under Leopold and
his sons. The conquest of Hungary during the counter thrust
after the Turkish siege of Vienna in 1683 had transformed
the old imperial residence—hitherto a threatened border town
in the extreme eastern part of the Empire—into the center
of a new and growing major power on the Danube, while
at the same time Louis XIV's advances to the Rhine and
the later struggle for the Spanish inheritance (conducted
at first behind the scenes and on the diplomatic level)
focused attention on the west. Leopold did not find it easy
to ally himself with the Protestant maritime powers, England
and the Netherlands, and he was deeply indignant at the
Pope's overtures to France. But in both instances he recognized the changed world situation and drew the proper
conclusions. He waged war along the Rhine to preserve imperial territory from the clutches of the French, and, even while
fighting the Hungarian malcontents and the Turks in the
east, he had to reckon with the machinations of French
diplomacy. But his victory over the Turks, fulfilling his ancestors' century-old longing, reinforced his belief in the election of the House of Habsburg.

Though he was a less remarkable statesman than his great
antagonist, the Sun King, and originally far inferior in

strength, he dared to enter the battle for the Spanish inheritance against his cousin (for Louis XIV was also the son of a Spanish Habsburg mother). But in the middle of the struggle, and after almost fifty years of rule, Leopold died.

His son and successor, Emperor Joseph I, seems to have been very different, even in appearance, for he was one of the few old-Habsburgs without the typical Habsburg lip. His tutor, Wagner von Wagenfels, found a receptive listener for his history lessons, lessons that were imbued with a passionate German nationalism. When the question of marriage came up Joseph said, "I do not want a French wife or any Latin kind of foreigner."

In matters of religion he seems to have been more tolerant than his father, for he forbade preachers to abuse the Protestants in any way. When the two Wittelsbach electors of Bavaria and Cologne were ceremonially condemned as enemies of the empire because of their alliance with France, he showed a proud imperial patriotism that harmonized with Habsburg interests. His clash with the Francophile Pope Clement XI—the last armed conflict of a German Emperor with the Pope—revived memories of the battles in the High Middle Ages, and at the end of the century Emperor Joseph II's contemporary admirers tried to see in the first Joseph a forerunner of their own liberal monarch. But in fact this was merely an episode in the middle of the War of the Spanish Succession. It was vital for the Emperor's younger brother, Charles, who had been chosen as the future Spanish King and who was fighting in Spain, that he be recognized in the Italian dependencies of the Spanish crown as the true sovereign. When the Pope could not make up his mind to this and even threatened to excommunicate Prince Eugene, who was encamped with his troops on papal territory, Vienna remembered that Comacchio, in the Po Delta, had once been an imperial fief, and occupied it. The Pope, left in the lurch by France, whose soldiers could not compete with the war-hardened imperial troops, thereupon saw himself forced to give in.

Joseph I was surrounded by an outstanding group of advisors, so that it is not easy for later historians to determine the Emperor's own share in the victories and successes of the wars that filled his brief six-year reign. The court historians called him "Joseph the Victorious." One thing is certain: when as Crown Prince he was understandably opposed to his father, he condemned the unwieldiness of his father's administration and showed himself willing to undertake a new, more energetic policy. To be sure, at first he sometimes lacked endurance and perseverance, and perhaps also the application necessary to manage affairs of state bureaucratically, though his youth and his understandable enjoyment of music, games, and dancing may excuse him. He thought of obtaining Bavaria for his House, an ambition later taken up again by his brother Charles as well as by Joseph II. When he died of smallpox in 1711, at the age of thirty-three, Spain again slipped out of the grasp of the German Habsburgs, since the maritime powers, England and the Netherlands, did not want to see Charles V's Empire reconstituted under Joseph's brother Charles. His contemporaries thought that a great hope of the House and the Empire had gone down into the grave.

Charles VI, who now acceded to the Empire and the Austrian patrimony, and who in the war had failed to achieve the Spanish crown but had gained the dependencies in northern and southern Italy and the southern Habsburg Netherlands, resembled his father Leopold more strongly in appearance than had Joseph, though in character he was more a seventeenth-century Spanish Habsburg, like Philip III and Philip IV. He had been so accustomed to living in the hope of being King of Spain that, even after the peace treaties of Utrecht, Rastatt, and Baden, which ended the War of the Spanish Succession, it was a long time before he could awake from his dream. His grief for his lost Spanish realm, that he was to have ruled as Charles III, took shape in his incomplete plan to build an Austrian Escorial at Klosterneuburg near Vienna.

Members of other nations at the imperial court complained for a long time about the excessive influence of Spanish counselors on the Emperor. But the experience of the sea that Charles had gained during his Spanish years awakened his interest in navigation and maritime trade, and thus stimulated the foundation of Austrian trading companies and promotion of the port of Trieste. But for the history of the House of Habsburg the most important positive event during the reign of the last old-Habsburg Emperor was the Pragmatic Sanction, issued in 1713, the year of the Peace of Utrecht. This domestic edict was to ensure the succession for Charles's daughters, as yet unborn, in preference to the daughters of Joseph I. It was the first declaration of the legal and political indivisibility of the "far-flung and splendid monarchy," as Prince Eugene called the Emperor's lands when he exhorted the future wearer of the imperial crown to fuse the domains into a "single entity." In this Pragmatic Sanction the principle of primogeniture (the right of sole inheritance by the eldest son or, if no sons existed, by the eldest daughter) was for the first time declared to be legally and politically binding on the German Habsburg line and finally eliminated the possibility of divisions of inheritance.

Charles did not, however, have a happy touch in his endeavors to secure recognition of the Pragmatic Sanction, and with it the succession of his eldest daughter, Archduchess Maria Theresa, born in 1717. The guarantee by the European powers was bought all too dearly with great political sacrifices, the abandonment of the Ostend Company, the participation in two luckless wars (the War of the Polish Succession and the Turkish war, when he was allied to Russia), and territorial losses in the south, west, and east.

After Charles's death events proved the accuracy of Prince Eugene's warning that power politics lay at the root of the whole problem.

The consequences of all too frequent intermarriage, which probably caused the extinction of the Spanish Habsburg line, can be recognized in a milder form in Charles VI, with whom the Austrian Baroque and the male line of the old-Habsburg dynasty came to an end. The great pastimes of the last old-Habsburgs—hunting, music, opera, and the noble art of horsemanship as practiced in the Spanish riding school—were also cultivated by him with a last, somewhat weary sophistication. In the plague year of 1713 (also the year of the Peace of Utrecht and the Pragmatic Sanction) the Emperor vowed a church to his patron saint, Charles Borromeo (the saint of plagues). The Viennese Karlskirche, the masterwork of Johann Bernhard Fischer von Erlach, was completed in 1737 (the year of Prince Eugene's death and three years before the Emperor himself died), and in it Austrian Late Baroque art created a last splendid glorification of the union of religious and political rule, of Habsburg imperial sway and triumphant Catholicism. It is a building of astounding unity in spite of its bold fusion of the most various elements, cupola, Grecian temple façade, Roman triumphal columns, and bell towers, and it is comparable to the Empire of these last old-Habsburgs, in whom the most divergent historical traditions seem united in a sort of pre-established harmony.

12: The Great Empress

Maria Theresa, the daughter of Charles VI and a Guelph wife (Princess Elizabeth-Christine of Brunswick-Lüneburg-Wolfenbüttel), was the last old-Habsburg; with her ended the line of Habsburg rulers that had started more than five hundred years earlier with King Rudolf. But the ancestress of the new house of Habsburg-Lorraine was, both in herself and in her achievements, much more of a beginning than an end. She was a true founder, for she created a new state and maintained it with the help of outstanding counselors and assistants, who had been most fortunately chosen from her inherited domains, and she defended it against external enemies with intelligence and fortitude. She developed a new style of sovereignty and a new relationship between the ruler and his people. With this motherly monarch, who ordered that her tutor, the Countess Fuchs, be buried in the family vault (*Kapuzinergruft*—vault of the Capuchins) in Vienna— the only non-Habsburg to receive the honor—the "bourgeois" age of the dynasty began. She eliminated the invisible "forbidden zone" that ever since the days of Charles V had surrounded the person of a Habsburg ruler in Vienna—increasingly after Maximilian II's sons had been educated in Spain, though the German Habsburgs were never so unapproachable as the Spanish. Like her ancestors Rudolf I and Maximilian I, Maria Theresa became truly popular with her subjects, and there are innumerable anecdotes about her.

Her husband, Francis Stephen of Lorraine, had to surrender his patrimony of Lorraine for the Grand Duchy of Tuscany in order to win the hand of the Habsburg heiress, since after the War of the Polish Succession it was the only way for the *Hofburg* to obtain a French guarantee for the Pragmatic Sanction—a guarantee later proved worthless. "No surrender, no Archduchess," shouted Johann Christoph, Baron von Bartenstein,[1] at the Duke of Lorraine. Charles VI had had to promise England that only a prince with little power of his own should receive the hand of the heiress to the throne. The union therefore lay under the shadow of high European politics, yet from the start it was a love match and one of the happiest royal marriages of the time.

Though the genealogists of the House of Habsburg had long since abandoned the old fantastic legends, under the stimulus of historical criticism they welcomed the new House of Habsburg-Lorraine as if it were the story of Eticho over again, and the reunification, after almost a thousand years, of two lines of the old Lotharingian ducal House. In contrast to Charles VII, who briefly annexed the imperial office for the Wittelsbachs, the Lotharingian as Emperor and husband of a Habsburg was not felt to be making any breach in the unbroken tradition of three centuries of Habsburg imperial rule, and in popular sentiment, as in common usage, the Habsburg-Lotharingians always remained "the Habsburgs."

Habsburg marriages with German princesses in the two preceding generations closely connected Maria Theresa with the German princely Houses. In contrast to Emperor Maximilian I—whom contemporaries and successors regarded as particularly German, although he was the son of a Portuguese princess, the grandson of a Polish princess, and the great-grandson of an Italian princess, and had relatively few German ancestors—Maria Theresa had a strong preponderance of Germans in her family tree. She and her children barely showed the typical Habsburg physical characteristics,

[1] The leading statesman during Charles VI's last years, and Maria Theresa's counselor in the first stormy period of her reign, he was later the tutor of Joseph II.

although Francis Stephen, through his grandmother, Archduchess Mary Eleanor, was also a great-grandson of Emperor Ferdinand III. The characteristics reappeared again in the following generation, with Leopold II's children, probably because the old-Habsburg bloodline had been reinforced by their mother, a Spanish Bourbon.

How much of the great breach that Maria Theresa made in the old-Habsburg tradition (while carefully preserving certain external forms and ceremonies) was due to her descent, or to her husband's influence, and how much to the influence of her advisors and, later, of her son and co-regent Joseph, or how much to the general tendencies of the age, is naturally a difficult and almost unanswerable question.

For this Empress was a great reformer, even a revolutionary, though a revolutionary with delicacy of feeling, feminine charm, an unerring instinct for the practicable, and a virtuoso's talent for the selection and treatment of collaborators. No ruler before or after her in the long line of the old-Habsburg or Habsburg-Lorraine dynasties understood as well as she how to put the right man in the right place at the right time; no one else, in the midst of exhausting wars, could have carried through so many and such revolutionary innovations, which later proved their effectiveness. A study of any aspect of modern Austrian history—public administration, finance or economic policy, public education, military organization, jurisprudence, or public health—leads to the inevitable conclusion that the most energetic reforms and the most beneficent institutions date back to the reign of the great Empress.

Her hidebound Lord High Steward complained, with some justification, of "the unfortunate spirit of innovation, which put in an appearance soon after the demise of Emperor Charles VI and daily increased," and of the "total upheaval and refashioning of the most illustrious Arch-house's form of government, which had been traditional ever since the very beginning and for so many centuries." But what is most remarkable is that the Empress, besides carrying out her work of reform in the face of the persistent survival and dogged opposition of century-old traditions and sacred privileges, besides struggling to preserve her inheritance, and worrying over the course of major European politics, still found time to be a model wife and bring sixteen children into the world ("One cannot have enough of them, in this matter I am insatiable," she once wrote to one of her daughters-in-law), as well as to take exemplary care of their education and upbringing.

An official document in the Vienna House, Court, and State Archives illuminates the character of this unusual woman perhaps better than all encomiums, and at the same time illustrates how she differed from the earlier Habsburgs. Once, when she was reading state papers at breakfast and probably, like a true Viennese, had dipped her *croissant* into her coffee, she made a coffee-spot on a document. Immediately she drew a circle around it with her pen and wrote that she was very much ashamed of having made it. Goethe, using eye-witness reports, described in his *Dichtung and Wahrheit* the engaging impression that the Empress made during her husband's coronation in Frankfurt. In addition to such anecdotes, her letters (particularly those to her daughters living in foreign courts, but also to her generals and ministers) reveal such freshness, warmth, and native common sense, that one can catch a little of the enchantment cast by this motherly woman even after her original beauty had been destroyed by many childbirths, mental and physical hardships, anxieties and excitements, and even after her husband died in 1765 and she mourned for him in lifelong and unquenchable grief.

At the very beginning of her reign Maria Theresa had to show courage in misfortune—perhaps the most important attribute in those destined to rule. When only twenty-three, she found herself surrounded by dangers, "without money,

without credit, without an army, without knowledge or experience, and also without advice, because each of the counselors wanted first of all to wait and see how matters would
turn out." Her exhortation to the despondent advisors is well-
known: "What gloomy goings on! Why such faces? You have
to talk, but help and advise the poor queen, instead of dis-
couraging her still more!" In her deeply moving letter to
Field Marshal Count Khevenhüller she wrote, referring to an
enclosed picture, "Here you have before your eyes a queen
and her son deserted by the whole world; what do you think
will become of this child?" The tale of her appearance in
Pressburg before the Hungarian Diet has been considerably
embroidered, but she was personally persuasive enough to
win from the Hungarian nobility a promise of greater assistance. Thus she succeeded in weathering the first great crisis
of her reign and preserving her inheritance intact during the
War of the Austrian Succession and the two Silesian Wars,
except for the loss of Silesia, Parma, and Lombard territories.

As Maria Theresa herself wrote in retrospect, until the
Peace of Dresden in 1745 she had "acted boldly, hazarding
everything," and had used all her energies. Then, just as
courageously, after the Peace had been concluded, she began
the great state reforms that had already been prepared during
the last years of the war, and started to remodel the complex of Austrian and Bohemian territories into a centralized
bureaucratic state.

In the Silesian Count Haugwitz she found an outstanding
collaborator who took over and developed the stimulating
model of Prussian administrative organization, creatively
adapting it to the conditions peculiar to Austria. As quite
often happens, the struggle between Austria and Frederick's
Prussia in the two Silesian wars and the Seven Years' War
led to a resemblance between the two enemies, a phenomenon observable elsewhere in history and all too often over-
looked. Both the bureaucracy and the Army, the two main-

stays of Maria Theresa's Austria, showed traits common to
or paralleled in the Prussian character. This bureaucratic-
military style later influenced Joseph II and, through him, the
Habsburg-Lorraine dynasty down to its last days. If bureaucratic and military soberness and unpretentiousness, complete devotion to duty, and subservience to the state are
taken as the essential old Prussian characteristics, then
Emperor Francis Joseph was far more "Prussian" than Emperor William II or many another romantic and imagina-
tively gifted offspring of the House of Hohenzollern. These
similarities between Austria and Prussia (for Frederick the
Great and Maria Theresa, though enemies, were both engaged
in domestic reforms) almost certainly arose because the two
countries are situated in the eastern part of Central Europe
and had to be constantly on the defensive against the east.
After Frederick's invasion of Silesia and Maria Theresa's resistance, the rivalry with Prussia (and later with the Germany
of William II) became vitally important in the attitude,
style, and ideology of the Habsburg dynasty.

Maria Theresa hated the great King of Prussia ardently
and from the bottom of her heart, not only because he was
"the robber of Silesia," but probably even more because the
cool, sharp, and ironic wit and temper of the "hermit of
Sans-souci" were so diametrically opposed to her own warm-
hearted, motherly, and wholly unintellectual character. One
of the great and painful disappointments in her life was her
growing awareness of traits of character and attitudes of
mind in her son Joseph that resembled those of Frederick,
the "evil man" and "ugly neighbor" whose falseness she had
always "abhorred," the "monster" that, as she wrote, "still
tortures us and so many thousands."

Her complaint against the cold irony and sarcastic wit of
the "philosophic century" was at the same time a protest
against the cast of mind of both her adversary and her son:

> The world is now so frivolous, so little benevolent. Everything is ridiculed . . . our Germans thus lose the best qualities they possessed—to be a little ponderous and rough, but straightforward, truthful, and diligent. For my part, I do not like anything that smacks of irony. Nobody is ever improved by it, but simply irritated, and I think it irreconcilable with loving one's neighbor.

Desperately, she entreated her son not to "lapse into a tone that, from the outset, banishes all tenderness, warmth, and friendship." Where all humanity and mutual sympathy are excluded, what sort of life is left? "They [people of this sort] are intellectual coquettes; a *bon mot*, a pun takes hold of them . . . they use it at the first opportunity, without thinking much whether it is appropriate or painful." She felt that lack of religious zeal was to blame for her son's intellectual attitude and urged him, from her anxious mother's heart, to attend more eagerly and devoutly to his religious duties.

Hatred for the King of Prussia finally led Maria Theresa and her chancellor, Prince Kaunitz, to an alliance with the old hereditary enemy, the French monarchy. The marriage of the young, easy-going Marie Antoinette to the French Dauphin was supposed to end forever the traditional Franco-Austrian hostility and the rivalry of the Houses of Habsburg and Bourbon. But the marriage was ill-starred, and the expected political advantage did not materialize. Neither France's nor Russia's help regained Silesia for Austria in the Seven Years' War, and Marie Antoinette's life in Versailles was a source of constant anxiety to her mother. Only just before she was guillotined in the French Revolution did Marie Antoinette prove, by her bearing and courage, that she was a daughter worthy of Maria Theresa.

The Empress herself was torn between maternal anxiety, sense of family, dynastic interests, and political plans on behalf of the daughters she had married into European princely families. Though such marriages were arranged only for dynastic and political reasons, the Empress's letters to her daughters in distant lands contained mostly personal advice and expressed her own worries and admonitions. She sometimes seemed to reveal a subconscious sense of guilt and sadness because political and dynastic interests forced her to send her daughters to foreign courts in distant countries, to marry men they did not love. For the Empress was a real child of the bourgeois and sentimental age, whose standard of values conflicted with the traditions and requirements of the dynastic idea. So she warned her daughters to adapt themselves to the taste of their new countries, in order to win confidence, and not to cultivate a dislike or a preference for any particular nation, since each had its good and bad points. "Remain a German at heart, if only in uprightness of character, but appear a Neapolitan in everything morally neutral, though in nothing that is evil," she wrote to her daughter Maria Josepha, who was to marry the King of Naples. And she advised her daughter Maria Amalia, who plagued her husband, Ferdinand of Parma, with not unprovoked fits of jealousy:

> The more you reveal your feelings and your trust in leaving your husband free, the more devoted he will be. All happiness in marriage consists of trust and constant kindness. Foolish love is soon past, but you must respect each other, and wherever possible be useful to each other. Each must prove the other's true friend, in order to be able to bear the misfortunes of life and to establish the welfare of the House. . . . All marriages would be happy if only one would conduct oneself like that.

The old naïve identification of political with family ties and values within the dynastic concept was threatened from two sides in the eighteenth century: politically, by the concept of an autonomous state and public weal independent of the ruler, yet commanding his obedience; humanly, by the feeling that the ruler and his family also had a right to their own personal happiness. The two were connected because the inevitable personal sacrifices that the ruler had to make were justified by the idea of service to the state. The difficulties that dominated the lives of many members of the Habsburg dynasty, as well as those of other European dynasties after the French Revolution, the conflict between the duties of sovereignty and private happiness—the image of the royal crown as a crown of thorns and a heavy burden, a concept alien to most earlier Europeans rulers—began to make themselves felt during Maria Theresa's life.

This conflict was particularly clear in the Empress's attitude to religion and the Church. As the daughter of a Guelph Protestant who had been converted to Catholicism before her marriage to the Emperor, she was a strict Catholic. The idea of religious toleration, which her son wanted to see victorious, was personally alien to her. Nevertheless, she became a great reformer in ecclesiastical policy, as in so many other spheres. Under Maria Theresa a new age of "Catholic Enlightenment" and *Josephinismus* superseded the Catholicism of the Baroque.

The pious and orthodox Empress restricted the number of pilgrimages and processions, set up obstacles to the foundation of new monasteries (making it in fact almost impossible), prohibited under threat of prosecution the taking of monastic vows before the age of twenty-four, and, most important, abolished the clergy's exemption from taxes. She forbade visitations by papal legates and, finally, although with a heavy heart, agreed to the expulsion of the Society of Jesus from Austria.

Though many of Maria Theresa's ecclesiastical measures appeared only to continue the old-Habsburg tradition of a state church, her reasons for them were appreciably different. Previous policy had been based on the sovereign's position as steward and protector of the Church. Kaunitz and Von Swieten, Maria Theresa's ecclesiastical advisors, and later Joseph II, were motivated not only by Jansenist and Febronian ideas but also by consideration of the welfare of the state and its subjects, and by utilitarian and commercial, political, and economic reasons for limiting the number of feast days and pilgrimages and curtailing ecclesiastical pomp. A certain tension began to make itself felt in ecclesiastical policy between the ruler's personal devoutness (still very evident in Joseph II) and the already wholly secularized ideas of reasons of state and the public good. The dynasty's consciousness of its special relationship to God and the Church, as divinely chosen for its purpose and also responsible to God for the spiritual welfare of its subjects, continued to find expression in the ruler's life as well as in his policy, but less and less forcefully. Naturally, belief in the *Pietas Austriaca*, the special form of Habsburg piety, also waned.

Maria Theresa herself was still firmly attached to the religious and dynastic ideas of her ancestors. Looking back on the precarious situation in which she had found herself on her accession, she regarded her salvation exclusively as God's work and a "miracle" ("All this I firmly believe was allowed by the Almighty to prove to everyone, but especially to me, that my salvation was due to him alone; and being convinced of this in my heart . . . :" "I ascribe this by no means to my virtue but exclusively to God's Grace . . . ;" "when God's strong arm began to make itself clearly felt on my behalf . . . ," etc.). In her state papers the Empress again and again mentioned the *Pietas Austriaca* and also the *Clementia Austriaca* as the "chief pillars" of her rule. But at the same time, quite naïvely and almost unconsciously, a note of criticism of these venerable basic concepts of Austrian traditional government crept in. The invocation of ancestral piety and God-fearing ancestors, the urgent admonition to her successors to continue cultivating and exalting the Habsburg virtues were followed by the statement that further donations to churches and monasteries were at the least superfluous, in fact even harmful, in the "German patrimonies," which were in any case completely reconverted. The "House of Austria's native clemency and leniency" were so often mentioned as having weakened "sovereign authority" that they almost unconsciously acquired the connotation of worn-out custom and slovenliness.

The Empress was certainly aware that "many of my forebears have been accused of all too dilatory deliberation or indecision in the affairs of state and of their country." Once she even wrote, ". . . which truth I have had daily set before my eyes and have fully comprehended, that I do not belong to myself but only to the public," suggesting the later idea of the monarch as servant of the state. Probably no royal writings contain a more unpretentious and moving passage than the following in which the strength and greatness of soul both of the mother and the ruler become apparent:

> And however much I love my family and my children, so much that I would not spare myself effort, trouble, anxiety, or work, yet I would have preferred to them the country's general good if I had been persuaded in my conscience that I could further it or that the well-being of my subjects required it, seeing that I am the general and chief mother of my country.

The possibility of a conflict (alien to dynastic thought in earlier times) between the ruler's "private" sense of family and his duty as "father or mother of the nation"—an honorific title that Maria Theresa often and gladly claimed for herself—is here clearly expressed.

All these developments only began to make themselves felt with Maria Theresa. She overcame the conflicts that could have resulted from them, both for herself and for the state, by focusing her unspeculative mind entirely on practical matters, exercising her strong personality, and bringing to bear her most dominant characteristic, motherliness, in the political sphere. The public, the dynasty, and the family were equally dominated by the lively presence of the mother, who was at one and the same time head of the dynasty, mother of her large family, and mother of her country, and on whose person all the sentimental energies of her subjects, freed by the repression and curtailment of Baroque piety, now concentrated. Here perhaps lay the deepest reason for the powerful effect that Maria Theresa, great imperial mother of Austria, exerted on her contemporaries and on posterity.

13: Servants of the State

On February 10, 1861, at the beginning of Austria's constitutional era, Archduke Albert, the senior member of the House of Habsburg-Lorraine and the most outspoken representative of the purely dynastic ideas that had motivated the old-Habsburgs in previous centuries, wrote a detailed memorandum of his views on the position of the dynasty. Though addressed to Francis Joseph's Adjutant General, Count Crenneville, it was really directed at the Emperor himself.

> The great Maria Theresa, that fine judge of men, who was so loved and honored by her subjects that we are still living off the legacy she left, knew very well why she exalted her family as much as possible and thus procured them respect and esteem throughout the world. By setting them apart and keeping them united, she as far as possible concealed the weakness of individuals from the nation's gaze and from destructive criticism, and the aura surrounding her family raised her many degrees in the estimation of her subjects. Her brilliant son, Joseph II, wanted only to be respected and loved for his own sake, as a human being. He forgot that no throne can maintain itself without an aura, and after ten years he died broken-hearted, leaving the empire in a state of ferment, and partly in open rebellion. His dictum that he considered himself the *first civil servant* regretably still haunts many minds today.

The essential difference between Maria Theresa's and Joseph's concepts of the state and of the ruling House, as seen from the nineteenth-century point of view, is here clearly worked out. If, however, one approaches the great Empress as we have done, after a survey of the previous history of the dynasty, and comes to her by way of her old-Habsburg ancestors, one notices first of all the increasingly bourgeois manner of life, the abandonment or at least curtailment of the Burgundian-Spanish ceremonial in the personal conduct of the ruler and her family—defenders of the old customs complained of the "dreadfully truncated etiquette"—and her spontaneous friendliness when dealing with subordinates. Under the Empress not a trace remained of the majestic and solemn bearing of the old-Habsburgs, which had extended to all the insignificant details of human existence (the scurrilous anecdotes about Leopold I had been delightedly seized on by the sarcastic cynic Frederick the Great), and which had still very largely dominated court life under Charles VI.

Maria Theresa's feeling for the majesty, election, and special position of her House and all its members was still dominant, though completely unsophisticated and matter of fact, and she expressed it frequently in her letters and admonitions of her children, especially Archduke Ferdinand, whose predilection for artists, musicians, and comedians she repeatedly censured. In spite of her humanity and warmth, the highest political value for her lay in the Arch-house, not in the state or the concept of fatherland, which were completely alien to her. Even the time-honored Holy Roman Empire she could understand only in relation to the Habsburgs, as is shown by her proceedings against the Wittelsbach shadow Emperor, Charles VII. She was firmly convinced that God's grace rested on the Arch-house, because in retrospect she could see that crises and dangers had been happily overcome since her accession.

The Empress's sons, Joseph and Leopold, were already filled with the King of Prussia's idea of being servants of the state; as pupils of the Enlightenment and of Rationalism they were no longer, like their mother, automatically convinced of the divine right of the House and their peculiar elevation above all other mortals. They saw the justification of their position—which they certainly believed in upholding

—only in service to the state and to the welfare of their subjects, in line with the prevailing theory of the social contract.
The metaphysical grounds for sovereignty were replaced by
rationalist and utilitarian theories. In the innumerable direc-
tives and programs for the education of princes that Joseph
and Leopold, as true sons of a century devoted to education,
wrote, they repeatedly stressed the necessity of convincing
royal children that they were ordinary mortals, not a whit
better than their subjects, and that their exceptional privilege
could be justified only by untiring work on behalf of their
people. The classic eighteenth-century theory of equality was
not more outspokenly formulated by the theoreticians and
drafters of programs for the American and French revolutions than in the instructions for the education of Habsburg
princes.

For example, Leopold II wrote that, in bringing up his children:

> No effort should be spared to inculcate in the princes a feeling for
> their country and respect for its special character. One should es-
> tablish in them a reluctance to impose taxes on the population,
> and kindle in them, as the only permissible passions, philanthropy,
> compassion, and the desire to make their subjects happy. One
> should develop in them sympathy for the poor, and ensure that they
> never prefer the rich to the poor. It is the greatest misfortune for
> a prince not to see things with his own eyes, and to be uninformed
> about the true state of affairs in his own country.

Another passage in the same document reads, "Above all else
princes must be persuaded that all men are equal," and
finally:

> Princes must always be conscious of their humanity; that they owe
> their position only to an agreement between other men; that
> they [the princes] in turn must perform all their duties and tasks,
> as rightly expected of them by other men, because of the advantages
> bestowed on them. Princes must always consider that they cannot
> degrade other men without degrading themselves.

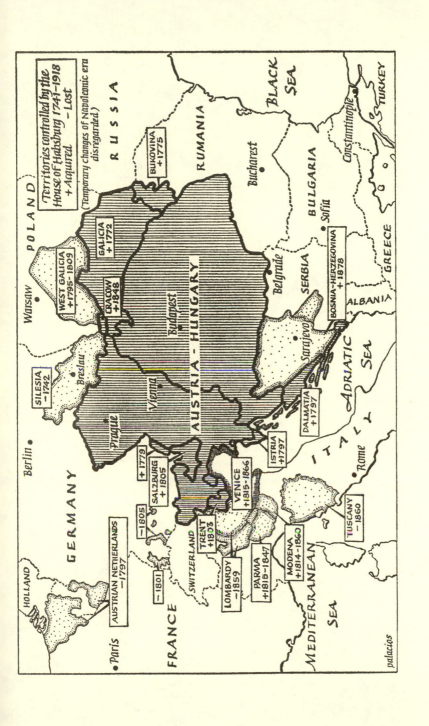

Territories controlled by the
House of Habsburg 1741-1918
− Lost   + Acquired
(Temporary changes of Napoleonic era
disregarded)

BLACK SEA

TURKEY

RUSSIA

POLAND

Warsaw

GERMANY

Berlin

HOLLAND

Paris

FRANCE

BUKOVINA +1775

RUMANIA

Bucharest

GALICIA +1772

WEST GALICIA +1795-1809

CRACOW +1848

SILESIA −1742

Breslau

Prague

Vienna

Budapest

AUSTRIA − HUNGARY

BULGARIA

Sofia

SERBIA

Belgrade

BOSNIA-HERZEGOVINA +1878

Sarajevo

ALBANIA

GREECE

Constantinople

+1779

SALZBURG +1805

−1805

AUSTRIAN NETHERLANDS −1797

−1801

SWITZERLAND

TRENT +1803

LOMBARDY −1859

PARMA +1815-1847

MODENA +1814-1860

VENICE +1815-1866

ISTRIA +1797

DALMATIA +1797

ADRIATIC SEA

ITALY

Rome

TUSCANY −1860

MEDITERRANEAN SEA

palacios

When Joseph II was criticized for throwing open the parks of Prater and Augarten to the Viennese public, he made the famous retort that, if he wanted to keep only to the society of his peers, he would have to incarcerate himself in the family vault of the Capuchins. This statement (taken together with Leopold II's instructions on education) marks perhaps the sharpest contrast to the concept of the necessary separation of the dynasty from the common people, as developed by Charles V and Philip II and advocated again in the nineteenth century by Archduke Albert.

No other Habsburg figure was and is the object of such widely divergent opinions as Joseph II. While some even try to deny that he was a reformer, others call him "the rebel in purple," and the "imperial revolutionary," and a modern English historian compares him to Lenin. Some stress his failure and his need to revoke part of his reforms, while others point to the deep and lasting traces left by his efforts in the style, method, and intellectual outlook of the Austrian bureaucracy, and indeed in the ruling élite of all the nations once subject to the Habsburg monarchy.

The word *Josephinismus*, coined to cover his ecclesiastical-political measures and ideas, was so far expanded in meaning that it finally embraced Austrian ecclesiastical policy as far back as the Middle Ages, or else well beyond the fall of the Habsburg monarchy. The concept has also been repeatedly redefined, depending upon whether the interpretation was made in terms of religion, philosophy, ecclesiastical policy, or state and national politics. For Austrian liberalism in all periods, Joseph was a national hero; for anticlericalism, the great "purifier of the faith"; for the German Austrians, especially in Bohemia and Moravia, "Joseph the German"; for radicals and democrats, the "People's Emperor" and the "Liberator of the Peasants"; for conservative Catholic circles, the "Enemy of the Church," the "vulgar rationalist," and "doctrinaire." While some historians have seen him as not very different from his mother and have stressed that he merely—and not very skillfully—continued the work of reform begun by Maria Theresa (endangering it by his rashness, obstinacy, and dogmatism more than he furthered it), others have pointed out that the germs of many an unpleasant institution in the period of Francis I, particularly relating to police and censorship, can be traced back to Joseph's epoch.

A significant ruler, Joseph was intellectually fashioned by the enlightenment and rationalism of his time. He combined a high ethical concept of his duties as sovereign with restless energy, bold planning and execution. But he underestimated the power of persistence in the opposition. Though he had deep insight into the needs of his time and the dangers of the future, he had very little empathy for any alien mentality and disregarded existing realities that had been determined by tradition, as well as spiritual imponderables. Joseph did not possess his mother's knowledge of people and sure political instinct. His psychological mistakes aroused opposition to his ecclesiastical as well as his national policies; the attempt to subject Hungary to the same centralist and bureaucratic system as that in the Austro-Bohemian lands foundered on Hungarian resistance and the unfavorable political situation abroad; and his attempt to pursue an energetic policy in the empire and to win Bavaria for his House was quashed by Frederick the Great's opposition.

But the ledger of failures is more than matched by a respectable balance of achievements and successes: the edict of toleration and the abolition of serfdom; the training of new types of civil servant and priest; colonization in Hungary and Galicia; basic legal, social, health, and educational reforms; the promotion of agriculture, trades, and industry; and the founding of the *Burgtheater* as a "German national theater," and of the *Allgemeine Krankenhaus* (General Hospital) in Vienna.

Undoubtedly the motive force that inspired Joseph's

achievements, and also caused his failures, was the idea of the monarch as servant of the state, whose duty is ceaseless devotion to his subjects' well-being. Since he was denied personal and family happiness (his much loved first wife and his child both died early, and his second marriage, entered into for political reasons, was unhappy), he became entirely absorbed in his work, while a certain emotional frigidity and autocratic harshness in his character became steadily more pronounced. He foresaw hard times for the Habsburg polity and tried to anticipate them by his reforms: the abolition of social inequalities, the improvement of popular education, general health, and the level of general welfare, and a standardization achieved through a centralized administration.

To bind together the various countries and nationalities, the Emperor created a dependable, German-speaking bureaucracy (devoted, like him, to the idea of service to the state), hierarchically organized to form a pyramid of achievement and merit, at whose apex stood the Emperor himself as the chief civil servant. In fact, this bureaucracy, partly created and partly refashioned by Joseph II, proved itself (along with the Army, which was imbued with a similar spirit) to be the most dependable prop and stay of the Habsburg monarchy until its fall. Thereafter, as one of the most valuable heirlooms of the old Empire, it served the Austrian Republic and the new states created out of the old monarchy after 1918. The successful and prosperous administration developed by Joseph in northern Italy, which is today acclaimed by Italian historians, was as much to the credit of Joseph's principles as the administration of the Grand Duchy of Tuscany, which Joseph's brother Leopold established on the same pattern, and which converted Tuscany into a model state in the Italy of that period.

Joseph II's reign marked such a deep cleft in the development of the Habsburg dynasty that, in spite of many later attempts, there was no possibility of return to the former concepts of sovereignty. With Joseph, the idea of the state as independent of the dynasty, and even superior to it, became consciously established in the patterns of thought of members of the imperial House. The notion was, however, difficult to reconcile with the historic character of the Habsburg monarchy and the intense differences between the individual countries and possessions, or with the old problem of tension between west and east, exemplified at the time by the difference between the Austrian and Bohemian territories and those of the Hungarian Crown of St. Stephen. For Joseph's effort to create a united Austrian state by incorporating Hungary into Maria Theresa's administrative structure failed as badly as the later attempt, made on the same principles and with the same means and purpose, after the Revolution of 1848–49 had been suppressed. Since the establishment of a single state did not succeed, the historical forces of opposition, stemming both from the nationalistic tendencies of the individual countries and from the dynasty itself, were able to develop much greater vitality and powers of resistance than they showed in other nations.

The whole history of the Habsburg dynasty and polity after Joseph II was therefore dominated by the struggle among conflicting tendencies. Powerful forces within the dynasty wished to reject the inheritance from Joseph and return to the old dynastic ideas of the monarchy. Attempts were made to replace the outworn concept of the dynasty's mission with new values and ideas that would enable it to retain its central position. Finally there was the continuing and unquenchable force of Joseph's concepts of the state, which always allied themselves with the elements working to conserve, form, or consolidate the nation (the economic and geographic realities of the Danube area, and the "Josephan" tendencies in the bureaucracy and the Army), and with the desire, common

to the liberal bourgeoisie and the democratic mass movements, for the formation of a true state.

In his "fanaticism for the welfare of the state," as he himself called it, Joseph II tried to convert the many faceted
monarchy into "a single province, equal in all its institutions
and responsibilities," and "a single mass of people all equally
subject to impartial guidance." "Our monarchy is large, un-
wieldy, and made up of very different countries. If all would
join hands together in good will and warm friendship, I might
still see the happy results, and I do not abandon hope that
it can be achieved if it is really desired and pursued with
determination." His lament anticipates Francis Joseph's
motto, "*Viribus unitis.*" But a new element appears in the
political thought of Leopold, Joseph II's young brother and
successor, and it clearly distinguishes his concept of the state
from that of his admired and criticized, loved and feared, elder
brother. As a docile pupil of Montesquieu and the Physiocrats, motivated by the new respect for the historical process
and historical individuality that was already awakening all over
Europe, Leopold did not allow his enthusiasm for reform
to keep him from always considering the historical singular-
ities and traditions of the different subject countries, or from
setting great store by the co-operation and approval of his
subjects, in contrast to Joseph's autocratic determination to
improve the world. He had a variety of constitutions drafted
for Tuscany; through new municipal constitutions he tried
to interest the citizens in co-operation and shared responsibility, and with his disbanding of the Army and Navy and his
pacifist policy of neutrality he earned the applause of the
European philosophers.

Shortly before his accession in Austria he wrote a letter to
his favorite sister, Maria Christine, Regent of the Netherlands,
in which he announced his basic political tenets in the form
of a creed. It was diametrically opposed to the old-Habsburg

concepts of sovereignty and also to those ideas that his own grandson, Archduke Albert, advocated almost a century later.

> I believe that the sovereign, even one who has inherited his position, is only the delegate and representative of his people, for whom he exists, and to whom he must devote all his work and care; I believe that every country should have a legally defined relationship or contract established between the people and the sovereign which limits his power, so that when the sovereign does not observe the law he actually forfeits his position (which is granted to him only under that condition) and it is no longer anyone's duty to obey him. I believe that the executive power belongs to the sovereign, but the legislative power to the people and their representatives, and that they may make new conditions with every change of sovereign. . . .

The briefness of Leopold's reign in Austria and the advent of the French Revolution (whose first stage Leopold, true to his principles, had honestly approved of) prevented his concepts of the state from having a more lasting effect in subsequent periods. His ideas bore abundant harvest only in the fortunate and successful work of his son, Archduke John, in Styria, and in his efforts to cultivate, preserve, and develop well tried traditions and create a new basis of trust between the people and the dynasty, while resisting the bureaucratic desire for regimentation. However, for the state as a whole and the dynasty as a whole, Leopold's developments and variations of the eighteenth-century concept of the state were not so significant as Joseph's enlightened absolutism.

The first great reaction to Joseph's ideas of the state began under his nephew Francis, who acceded in 1792, during the gathering revolutionary storms, after his father Leopold II, in his brief two-year reign, had ably resolved the governmental crisis inherited from Joseph. Francis, the eldest son of Leopold's large family (Leopold, like his mother, Maria Theresa, had sixteen children, and his sister, Maria Carolina of Naples, who most closely resembled her mother in political activity, eighteen) was in every way less gifted than his younger brother, Archduke Charles, the later victor of the Battle of Aspern and ingenious master of the theory and practice of war, or John the "Styrian Prince," who became German imperial regent in the stormy year of 1848.

In contrast to these two brothers, as outstanding in character as in intellect, Francis was narrow, prosy, reserved, and generally untalented. An explanation for his personality may perhaps be found in the vast superfluity of education and instruction to which Leopold's sons, and especially Francis, as future Emperor, were forced to submit from the days of their earliest childhood. Before this time the Habsburg education of princes had often proved too much of a good thing— Maximilian I had severe speech impediments as a child, evidently the psychological effect of his tutors' excessive zeal—but in the education-mad eighteenth century every reasonable limit was far overstepped. The evil was only aggravated when Francis moved from his father's court in Florence to the imperial court in Vienna, and was immediately apprenticed to his impatient and doctrinaire uncle, Emperor Joseph, who was equally admired and feared by his nephew.

The inevitable result of this upbringing was that Francis retreated even further into himself than his nature probably inclined him to do, and during the storms of the Revolution and the great conflict with Napoleon he clung passionately to the idea of the dynasty's exceptional position as his only dependable support; he fled back, as it were, into the shadow of the throne from which Joseph had firmly emerged. His political achievements, like those of his ancestor Frederick III, consisted chiefly in keeping his head above water in troubled times.

Like his Prussian contemporary and ally, Frederick William III, he distrusted intensely the forces of fervent nationalism that his brother Charles, in 1809, had tried to arouse and use in the war against Napoleon, because Francis instinctively and accurately recognized their revolutionary origin. This attitude was delightfully illustrated when he asked Castelli, the "patriotic poet" (in 1809, trembling before the advancing French), who on earth had ordered him to write patriotic poems. According to Francis, the citizen should be inspired to duty and sacrifice not by love of his country or the state, but by devotion and loyalty to the hereditary dynasty and the sacred person of the monarch.

Since the prosy bureaucratic son of the Enlightenment was no longer stirred by the majestic grandeur of the Baroque religious and political concept of the ruler, he replaced it with the image of the "worthy father of the family," "virtuous Emperor Francis," which he amply succeeded in embodying in his model conduct, his bourgeois plainness and conviviality, his exemplary home life, and even in his speech, which was tinged with Viennese dialect. Thus he became a classical personification of the patriarchal concept of the state, with all its good and bad points—a no longer completely native and original substitute for the metaphysically founded consciousness of mission among the old Habsburgs.

Francis preserved and further developed Joseph's bureaucratic system, partly because it suited his character, partly because its anonymity and lack of individuality afforded a welcome protection even to the monarch and thus assumed the function of the earlier "inviolable zone" or, in Archduke Albert's phrase, the "aura" of the old-Habsburgs. Although he rejected the concept of the autonomy of the state and its superiority to the dynasty, he was attracted by the possibility of evading unpleasant decisions and fobbing off annoying petitioners that was offered to him by the autonomy of the state apparatus and the fact that it was a law unto itself. Metternich's joke about "the Red Tapeworm," who bores his way in at one side of a bundle of state papers and emerges at the other without any effect except the resulting hole, acidly and exactly described the Emperor as bureaucrat.

By accepting the title of Austrian Emperor in 1804, and resigning that of Holy Roman Emperor in 1806, Francis completed the creation of the Austrian Empire and its detachment from the old universal bonds. Because he could not comprehend the emotional and historical values of the imperial tradition, or the mythological value of the Emperor and the Empire, he gave no more thought to a renewal of the *Sacrum Imperium* after the end of the Napoleonic wars. The last German and Roman Emperor was satisfied with the homegrown title of "Emperor of Austria." With the help of the bureaucracy that he had taken over from Joseph II he administered his Empire well, though it was still legally a complex of countries and domains ruled under different titles; and his encouragement of industry, in particular, earned him considerable acclaim. The long peaceful era after the Revolutionary and Napoleonic Wars, Francis's stoic calm and composure in all the vicissitudes of fate, and his consciously plain demeanor, all helped gradually to gain him remarkable devotion and sympathy from his subjects, although the best and most lively minds complained of intellectual stagnation and repression and idealized the figure of Joseph II in contrast to that of his nephew.

The personal blows that Francis had to bear—the deaths of his four wives and the anxieties caused by his children—helped him to win the sympathy of his subjects. It was not easy for him, after the defeat of 1809, to marry his daughter Maria Louise to Napoleon, because the fate of his aunt Marie Antoinette, the last Habsburg to marry a Frenchman, was all too horribly vivid in his memory and that of his contemporaries. Maria Louise's marriage, however, had a banal rather than a tragic end, for the insignificant Empress did not follow her husband into exile and soon found consolation elsewhere.

But the worst blow for the Emperor and the dynasty was the mental deficiency of the heir-apparent, the later Emperor

Ferdinand I (the first Austrian Emperor of that name, because a fresh enumeration began with the adoption of the
Austrian imperial title). Ferdinand's mother, Francis's second wife, was doubly related to her husband; her father (Ferdinand I of Naples and Sicily) was the brother of Francis's
mother, and her mother was the sister of Francis's father.
Although a younger son, Archduke Francis Charles (the
father of the later Emperor Francis Joseph), was fully capable of ruling, Francis and Metternich remained firmly in
favor of the sickly Ferdinand, in order to set an example of
the sacredness and inviolability of the principle of legitimate
succession. In reality, this stubborn attachment to principle
was a sign of weakness rather than of strength; at a time
when dynastic ideas retained their full vigor, Philip II
treated the parallel case of Don Carlos quite differently. The
preservation of a fiction did more harm than good to the
idea of the dynasty and to the polity itself, and it was small
consolation for Archduke Albert to write of Ferdinand's
reign, in the letter already quoted:

> Would Emperor Ferdinand's thirteen-year reign have been conceiv-
> able without the previously exalted and unimpeachable position of
> the ruling House? It could not have lasted a year. A monarchy that
> is to last for centuries must be so constructed that even weaker
> elements, which must be in the nature of things occur from time to
> time, can survive.

The difficulties created by such an obstinate adherence to
the established order of succession were most acutely emphasized because, at the time of the accession in 1835, the two
most outstanding sons of Leopold II (and brothers of the Emperor Francis), intellectually and morally Archduke Charles
and Archduke John, were still alive. The moral and intellectual greatness of Archduke Charles, the first conqueror of
Napoleon, belonged to a personality cast in the antique
mold. In his writings on military science (which in the con-
densed version alone comprise six volumes), he rewrought the

cataclysmic experiences of the Napoleonic wars in the spirit of German classical literature and philosophy, and in his three-volume study, *Grundsätze der Strategie* (*The Principles of Strategy*, 1813), he developed a theory of war that ranks with Clausewitz's later work and is perhaps superior to it in its inherent objectivity. His ability to be completely detached, as a critic of the art of war, was illustrated when a censor wanted to suppress an anonymously published volume of his work because of its excessively sharp criticism of the effectiveness of Charles's generalship! The same intense self-discipline with which he overcame the congenital ill-health that hindered his military career proved its worth when Napoleon, at Stammersdorf in 1805, tempted him with the offer of the Austrian throne, and later during the decades of his exclusion from responsible positions in military and political affairs.

The younger Archduke John, thirteenth child of Leopold II, was different but hardly less impressive. What Montesquieu and the Physiocrats had been for his father, Rousseau and the Romantics were for him. In conscious opposition to the "rotten" society at court, his admiration for the artlessness and simplicity of unspoiled mankind led him deliberately to seek and find close friendships with farmers and townspeople in the alpine regions, first in the Tyrol and then in Styria. He was a model landowner and *Radmeister*[1] in the Styrian Erzberg; he encouraged all branches of knowledge; he traveled for the sake of study and used the experience he collected, especially in England in 1815, to help the development of the Austrian economy; and as uncrowned "King of the Alps" he was as much admired by all Europe in the first half of the nineteenth century as his father had been in the second half of the previous one, when he was the model ruler of Tuscany.

[1] So called from the water wheel used to provide power in the smithy; the title was used by members of the Guild of Smiths and Ironworkers in the Erzberg.

Two closely connected predilections which recur in other members of the House during the subsequent epoch appear in John: a special love for Switzerland, as the cradle of the family; and the "flight of the middle class," a deliberate and conscious simplicity of dress, demeanor, and behavior. His love for Switzerland was first inculcated by his tutor, the historian Johannes von Müller. In a letter to Müller the seventeen-year-old prince described a visit in 1799 to a play that dealt with Engadine history, "What really pleased me was the praise given in the play to the Alpine people, and the confidence in their honor and loyalty. There is a battle in it in which the peasants beat the regular militia. Oh how I wished it were not a play!" When, in the last stage of the Napoleonic wars, he freed the city of Basel from impending danger by besieging and capturing the fortress of Hüningen, occupied by the French, the citizens of Basel and their fellow countrymen, as well as the Archduke himself, revived the memory of Rudolf of Habsburg. ("Old Rudolf must really rejoice to see how his descendant is wiping out all the old grudges and reconciling Austria and Switzerland, and how the latter wishes well to the House," wrote John in his diary.) He invited the Swiss pastor, Aegidius Scherer, to the ceremonial dedication of a cross on a peak of the Erzberg, on the grounds that "a Swiss can understand the feelings of a Styrian, but not so a plainsman or even a city dweller, for they have lost most of the old simplicity."

John's efforts to live the simple life, which also stimulated his interest in folk music and folk customs, and his research into dialect, were proverbial. "You know in any event, Paul, that with me everything is done simply and in grandfather's way," he wrote to his friend Paul Adler, a Styrian landowner, whose help he had asked in getting a milkmaid for his farm in Vordernberg. In another letter he very earnestly reproved his young wife, "Nani," because she had dressed Hiesel, the coachman, in a citified swallow-tailed coat for the trip to Graz.

When I introduced the gray coat into Styria, it was done to set an example of simplicity in manners; my household grew to resemble my gray coat, and so did my speech and my actions. The example took effect and the gray coat, disdained by some, recognized by the more virtuous, became a coat of honor and I will never put it off again; just as little will I give up my simplicity, I would rather give up my life. . . . If I had traveled about the country with the pomp that (I believe) is not necessary here, I should have had banquets, etc., given for me; I should never have learned the truth, never opened any man's heart, never have won the friendship of the virtuous. It is a serious matter that bears no trifling and that you should understand.

When one reads John's letters, or the enthusiastic descriptions of him written by Karl Ritter, the Berlin geographer, one understands the enormous popularity that he enjoyed, not only among the simple people in Styria and the Tyrol, but with the entire German middle class. This found visible expression when he was elected German imperial regent in 1848, and jubilation engulfed "Jack of Austria" on his journey to Frankfurt.

Leopold II, so unusual in many ways, had other outstanding sons besides Charles and John, the two most significant. The second eldest, Ferdinand III, Grand Duke of Tuscany, was exiled by the chaos of the Napoleonic era to rule briefly, first in Salzburg and then in Würzburg, before returning to Tuscany, where he governed for almost a decade according to his father's enlightened principles. He was able to educate his son and heir in the same spirit. Another son, Archduke Rainer, in spite of the limits imposed on his administration by the central authorities in Vienna, was similarly prosperous and successful throughout three decades as viceroy of the Lombardo-Venetian kingdom.

14: *The Crown of Thorns*

The revolutionary events of 1848, which threatened the existence of the Habsburg Empire, urgently demanded that the fiction of Emperor Ferdinand's reign be abandoned. Therefore on December 2, 1848, at the end of the "Year of Storms," the Emperor abdicated in favor of his eighteen-year-old nephew, Francis Joseph, the oldest son of Archduke Francis Charles and the energetic Archduchess Sophie, a native Bavarian princess. The popular joke that the word "WIR (We)," at the beginning of the new Emperor's first proclamation, was made up of the initials of Windischgrätz, Jellacić, and Radetzky, three generals who were fighting to suppress the revolutions in Austria, Hungary, and Italy, aptly characterizes the situation at the time of the young ruler's accession, only a month after the October rising in Vienna had been put down by Windischgrätz and Jellacić. Russian arms were needed to quell the Hungarian Revolution, while in Italy the aged Radetzky achieved a brilliant victory over Piedmont, which was allied to the Italian national revolutionary forces.

The first years of his reign—when the young prince was directed by an able statesman, Prince Felix Schwarzenberg, influenced by his mother Sophie, and advised by the former chancellor, Metternich, who remained in the background— were marked by a determined absolutist and centralist policy, in the hope that the whole state could be completely rejuvenated with the help of Joseph's bureaucracy. But after Schwarzenberg's death the policy formulated by Francis Joseph himself, which was not very adroit, isolated Austria from the rest of Europe during the Crimean War. And on the battlefields of the war of 1859 (against France and Pied-mont-Sardinia) Francis Joseph, though personally brave, lost confidence in his own military ability and the fortunes of war. Henceforth the neo-absolutist system of the first decades of his reign yielded to the liberal and nationalistic energies of a new period.

Austria's entry into the constitutional era, when the people themselves took a hand in shaping the destiny of their countries, acutely intensified the problem of the dynasty's function and position in a polity controlled by new forces. At that time Archduke Albert, who physically looked the part of an old-Habsburg, set down his basic tenets, in which he vigorously championed the old-Habsburg dynastic principles. In his criticism of a draft service regulation for the "k. u. k."[1] infantry, Albert objected to the replacement of *Archduke* by "Royal and Imperial Highnesses, Princes and Princesses of the Imperial House." He emphasized that the non-ruling members of the dynasty had been imperial princes only since 1804, after the establishment of the Austrian Empire, while for four hundred years

> they were the only people in the world to bear the title of Arch-duke, a title more ancient and therefore more highly esteemed than that of any Grand Duke or Prince Elector. An Archduke does not *de iure* yield precedence to these, only to a crowned head (Majesty), because the Austrian Archdukes, each one of whom is invested with the Archduchy, have never lost the privileges of rank due to them as ruling peers.

Primogeniture and entail had been established only in 1621 by Ferdinand II's will; though the rule of the younger sons ceased after the domains were no longer partitioned, their privileges of rank remained. Now liberals and democrats were trying to replace *Archduke* with the commonplace *Prince*,

---

[1] *Kaiserlich und königlich*—royal and imperial, i.e., pertaining to the entire Austro-Hungarian Empire until 1918.

"which every junior Salm or Leiningen,[2] etc., has a right to."

From these extremely important, not merely peripheral, questions of title and privilege Archduke Albert proceeded to a basic contrast between "dynasty" and "state":

> With what ideas, or confusion of ideas, about the ruling House are we inoculating the nations? How must the new classification strike the Army, which up to now (thank God!) was accustomed to serve, not the liberal and abstract concept of the *state*, but the *House* of Austria, as it were the embodiment of the fatherland, for which its members are supposed to bleed and die. Even now one hears old officers and soldiers saying, "I have served the House of Austria under two, three, or four emperors." This phrase expresses the essence of legitimacy, and the immortality of the dynasty. The dynasty, the *ruling House,* must be separated by a broad gulf from all its subjects; none of them, no matter how high he has risen, must be permitted to equal in external honors even the most junior member of the House. The *ruling House* has its own laws in the jointly formulated family statutes, the Emperor is the *Head* of the family, its judge, its sovereign, [and] the members must pay him obedience and respect and be his most faithful servants, setting a good example to the *subjects* everywhere; they themselves are not and cannot be *subjects* in the real sense of the word, because each of them has full claim to the throne in the established order of succession. It is exactly this order of succession that determines precedence among the individual members; apart from this and in relation to the subjects they are equal because of the rank that is theirs by birth, and only their Majesties stand high above this level. These are the principles on which, throughout four centuries, the House of Austria has grown strong, flourished, and become the oldest and most respected family in Europe. If these principles and this basis for continued existence were to be abandoned, the House would collapse and fall apart, confronted by a patched-together family of nations whose only bonds often were (and even now are) *the House and its Army,* and confronted by the democratic and leveling tendencies of the present day.

Here the Archduke added the already quoted passages on the contrast between Maria Theresa's and Joseph's ideas of

---

[2] Names of well-known minor German princes.

dynasty, monarch, and state, and of the way in which reigns "even of weaker elements," such as the reign of Emperor Ferdinand, could be sustained by strictly dynastic principles. Again and again he emphasized the necessity to safeguard the "absolutely exceptional position" of the dynasty by maintaining an "unbridgeable gulf" between the members of the Arch-house and their subjects. And at the end of this long disquisition he explained again that the assimilation of honors given to foreign princes and high-ranking subjects, to those reserved for the members of the ruling House, would be the first, most significant, and most decisive step "to a democratic and lawless course. This leads in the first or second generation to seeing the sovereign as the crowned executor of the people's will."

It was the sharpest and most decisive formulation of the dynastic principle that was still conceivable in the nineteenth century. Yet it contained clear evidence that the Archduke himself, who wished to bypass Joseph's idea of the servants of the state and return to the old-Habsburg concept of the dynasty, at the same time could not help being unintentionally influenced by the ideas that he opposed; for instance, in the revealing clause, "as it were the embodiment of the fatherland." In a manner completely foreign to old-Habsburg ideas he justified the function and position of the dynasty because of its service and importance to the ideal and concept of the "fatherland," and he even led up to the concept—dangerous to the purely dynastic philosophy—of the monarch as representative of the polity; he took over from Joseph von Hormayr the slogan of the "patched-together family of nations," developed as an antithesis to the romantic idea of organic political growth. With his passionate rejection of the ideas of a constitutional monarchy and the sovereignty of the people, Archduke Albert found himself in unusual agreement with the Viennese democrat and early Socialist Ernst Violand, who put forward in his *Sozialen Geschichte der Wiener Revolution* (*Social History of the Viennese Revolution*), published in 1850, the view that any other European dynasty might turn into a constitutional monarchy and recognize the principle of the people's sovereignty sooner than the Habsburg.

Archduke Albert and Archduke John, nephew and uncle, two nineteenth-century Habsburgs who did not wear the crown but, through rich political and military experience, possessed an exact knowledge of the polity and its problems, represented opposite points of view on the meaning of monarchy and the ways to safeguard and secure the dynasty, whose position they recognized as perilous. They were agreed only in their distaste for the bureaucratic concept of sovereignty, "monarchy as officialdom," whose adoption in Greece, for example, Archduke John sharply and accurately criticized during his travels there. But while John recommended safeguarding the dynasty by new and closer links with the middle class and the peasants, Albert could see salvation only in re-establishing of the old-Habsburg separation of the dynasty from its subjects.

An uncomplicated person, Emperor Francis Joseph basically shared Archduke Albert's sharply defined versions of the inherited dynastic ideas. But the Emperor's formative years (since he was some thirteen years younger than the tougher, more rigid and uncompromising Archduke) had coincided with the epoch-making Revolution of 1848–49 and its aftermath, and this helped him to absorb more easily, and therefore in much greater quantity, the new views of state and fatherland. Francis Joseph's chosen motto, "Viribus unitis" (with united strength), which expressed the idea of co-operation between the various nations of the Habsburg Empire, and of these nations with the dynasty, was at variance with a purely dynastic philosophy.

In the years of struggle for German hegemony (during which the monument to Archduke Charles, father of Archduke Albert, was set up in Vienna's *Heldenplatz* [Heroes' Square], with an inscription reading, "To the steadfast fighter for Germany's honor"), Francis Joseph felt himself to be an entirely "German prince"; espoused nationalism; and for its sake took part in the war against Denmark (1864) for possession of Schleswig-Holstein. But after the defeat at Königgrätz (July 3, 1866) had finally robbed Austria of her position in Germany and Italy and confined her to the Danube area, the Emperor drew closer and closer to the view already formulated by the great teacher and leader of the Czechs, Francis Palacky, in his letter of refusal to the Frankfurt National Assembly, written in the spring of 1848. The existence of the multinational Habsburg monarchy was justified, even indispensable, "in the interests of Europe, and of humanity itself," as the only sure protection against "the immeasurable and unutterable evil of a universal Russian monarchy," and as home and refuge for the small nations of Central Europe.

In this theory—which was supported after 1866 in the new Empire of Austria-Hungary with arguments drawn from world and national politics, ethics, economics, geography, and history—the dynasty and the throne retained their central position. Apart from the imperial army and diplomatic service, they provided the only bond uniting the two parts of the Empire; the highest authority, placed above nationalities and parties; the unifying keystone. The older, purely dynastic idea of the divine mission entrusted to the ruling House fused with Joseph's idea of the servant of the state, and Francis Joseph believed heart and soul in the new amalgam. It consecrated and justified his eighty-two years of existence and sixty-eight years of reign, a life full of appalling catastrophes and finally almost completely taken up with his "desk and document treadmill" (about which the monarch had already complained to his mother when he was only twenty-three). And the concept was confirmed rather than denied by later developments in the Danube area.

The moral worth, empirical justification, and posthumous confirmation of the idea should not blind us to its weaknesses and inherent contradictions; it also lacks the splendid compactness of the old metaphysical concept of the dynasty. The multiplicity of valid arguments that were adduced to justify the existence of the Danubian monarchy betrays at least the subconscious conviction, that the polity was threatened and beset by problems, and that it was anomalous in its own time. The members of the dynasty who were heads of state and could survey the whole Empire felt the threat and the problems more acutely than most other citizens. Thus the whole period of Francis Joseph's reign, in spite of its glitter and its achievements, the boom during the years when the *Ringstrasse* was built, the progressive and model social policy, and the growing participation of popular democratic movements in the government, also encouraged deeply pessimistic comments by members of the dynasty on the future of the Empire and its ruling House.

As far back as 1848 Archduke John, who was not only the most popular nineteenth-century Habsburg but also the most knowledgeable about the people's thoughts and feelings, had wondered if the future in Europe, too, belonged to republicanism. Throughout his long and eventful life Francis Joseph revealed a deeply rooted pessimism. Repeatedly, and particularly at the turning points in his life and in Austrian history, he used almost the same phrases about defending a hopeless position, fighting to the last breath, and dying with honor, which fitted his chivalric and straight forward nature. In his will he made provision for the possibility that "the crown might not remain in our House," and expressed the wish that his daughter Gisela take her legacies into her own hands because "they would be more secure in Germany than in Vienna." His description of himself to Theodore Roosevelt, as "the last European monarch of the old school," is tinged with the same skepticism and with a delicately ironic view of himself. And at the end of his life he told an Austrian diplomat that, "I have known for a long time how much of an anomaly we are in today's world."

Certainly in the last decades before the First World War the Austrian élite hoped afresh that the monarchy would be rejuvenated and the irksome nationalist struggles resolved. The Emperor himself had hoped, through granting universal suffrage and thereby integrating the masses into the state, that he would be able to provide a counterpoise to the bourgeois-liberal nationalism of lawyers and professors. The hope was rapidly proved vain, because the masses fell prey to a nationalism much more radical and robust than the humanistically tempered variety of the educated classes. The younger generation's wish for a basic and thorough reconstruction of the state centered on the person of the heir apparent, Francis Ferdinand. The discord between him and the Emperor, between "Belvedere" and "Schönbrunn,"[3] finally dominated domestic policy during "the last decades of a Great Power."

The Emperor was burdened with years; his inherited reluctance to make important decisions and take radical steps was aggravated by a long life of defeats and failures; he possessed much insight into the precarious situation of the Empire entrusted to him. Confronting him was an heir impatiently waiting for his hour to strike, who became almost desperate when he was forced to sublimate his urge for action into the hatching of plans, and when he realized that he must watch helplessly while precious time was running out and his future inheritance was falling apart. Francis Ferdinand saw the danger and problems of the state as well as the Emperor, but, being a younger and stronger man and a typical member of

[3] Two very impressive Baroque palaces in Vienna, residences of the imperial family, at this time inhabited by Francis Ferdinand and the Emperor respectively.

his generation, which relied too much on power and the triumph of will, he believed that radical measures could provide salvation at the eleventh hour. In contrast to many of the superficial optimists in his entourage and elsewhere in public life, who believed that a magic formula could transform the double monarchy into a free and peaceful partnership of nations, Francis Ferdinand realized the dangers that could arise from putting his ideas into practice. He foresaw the possibility of civil war and foreign intervention. There is no more deeply moving and prophetic statement in Habsburg history than the Archduke's that the Habsburg crown is a martyr's crown, and no one should strive for it who is not born to it.

This statement was made when Francis Ferdinand had attempted to obtain rights of legitimate inheritance for the sons of his morganatic marriage to Countess Chotek and had been refused. Like his whole attitude to his wife and children (he was an affectionate and considerate husband and father, as were almost all the members of his House), it reveals the tension between the idea of duty to the monarchy and its "exceptional position," and the desire for a quiet, bourgeois, happy life for oneself and one's family which, starting with Maria Theresa and Joseph II, was to dominate the dynasty's history increasingly after the middle of the nineteenth century. It was a conflict between responsibility to and feeling for one's family, between dynastic duty and personal inclination, which occurred more and more frequently.

Even in the sixteenth century, the golden age of the old-Habsburg dynastic concepts, when the idea of racial purity was exaggerated to the point of incest, Archduke Ferdinand of the Tyrol had made a love match with Philippine Welser. But it was an unheard-of event when Archduke John, in the first half of the nineteenth century, married, with the Emperor's permission, the daughter of the postmaster in Aussee, Anna Plochl (who was later, in 1844, created Countess of

Meran). In the second half of the nineteenth century and at the beginning of the twentieth, members of the dynasty's numerous branches started a veritable flight from the pressures of court etiquette and family statute, whose watchdogs were the Emperor and Archduke Albert (understandably very unpopular with the younger archdukes because of his strictness). The exceptional position of the dynasty was felt more and more as an oppressive burden that prevented one from leading a happy private life. This was the real reason for the tragedy of the highly gifted but unstable Crown Prince Rudolf (quite apart from the constitutional weakness inherited from his mother and the consanguinity of his parents). His opposition to his father's political views only set off the catastrophe.

Even Emperor Francis Joseph himself, who sacrificed his entire life on the altar of duty and to the idea of serving the state, longed in his heart of hearts for peaceful, middle-class happiness in simple, modest circumstances. This was expressed in his preference for a simple uniform, for plain dress, and for the hunting costume already favored by Archduke John, as well as in the deliberately plain furnishings of his living quarters in all his palaces—just an iron bedstead and a washbasin.

The Emperor's letters to the *Burgtheater* actress Katharina Schratt (in whose company he found the middle-class warmth, love, and comfort denied him in his marriage to his much admired but eccentric and restless wife, who reacted quite differently to the compulsions of court ceremonial) reveal a touching desire for at least an occasional release from a burden that oppressed him perhaps even more than it did those other members of the House who rebelled openly. By abdicating from the privileges of their position they simply laid down their responsibilities and escaped to a middle-class existence under middle-class names. That even Francis Ferdinand, in spite of his exalted ideas of the ruler's duty and his office, married beneath him and submitted to a tedious struggle for his married happiness shows how, in spite of individual differences, the basic problem was the same for all the various members of the dynasty. When the Emperor's granddaughter, the only child of his unfortunate son Rudolf, finally found her life's happiness with a socialist politician, it was only the most extreme form of the "flight from the imperial purple," the attempt to bridge the "unbridgeable gulf," whose preservation at any price had been demanded by Archduke Albert.

It is curious to see how the last generation of the ruling Habsburgs reverted so determinedly to the simplicity of their ancestor, Rudolf, who is reported to have patched his own doublet when on military expeditions and to have pulled up a turnip from the field when he was hungry. The love of middle-class simplicity helps to explain the sympathy for middle-class, republican Switzerland, which Francis Joseph also felt. It was a great Swiss historian, Jakob Burckhardt, a contemporary of Francis Joseph, who wrote the most penetrating characterization of the House as a whole since Rudolf of Habsburg: "physically by no means paragons; almost no genius; but goodwill, seriousness, deliberateness; endurance and equanimity in misfortune; no scoundrels and no slovens."

One of the most popular, and in appearance and behavior one of the most impressively aristocratic figures of the last Habsburg generation was Field Marshal Archduke Eugene, who after 1918 lived for fifteen years in Basel (which was intimately associated with Rudolf and the rise of the family, as well as being Jakob Burckhardt's native city), and was loved and appreciated by the inhabitants who knew him as "Erzi (Archy)."

The feeling that the crown was a martyr's crown, and a crown of thorns, was intensified for these generations, especially for Francis Joseph himself because of the series of catastrophes and tragedies in his immediate family. Almost contemporary with the defeat at Königgrätz and the recon-struction of the Austrian Empire as the Austro-Hungarian monarchy (a turning-point in the history of Habsburg sover-eignty and in Francis Joseph's life), was the tragic fate in the New World of his younger brother, Archduke Maximilian, who became Emperor of Mexico. The Archduke, imagina-tive, poetically gifted, and at first much more popular than Francis Joseph (a remarkable repetition of the contrast be-tween Frederick III and Albert VI, Charles V and Ferdinand I, Joseph I and Charles VI, and Francis I and Archduke Charles), had let himself be inveigled into the Mexican adventure by Napoleon III. Maximilian's life ended on June 19, 1867, before a firing squad in Querétaro. His wife Charlotte, a Belgian princess, went mad. The great Italian poet Giosué Carducci, in a fine poem on Castle Miramar on the Gulf of Trieste (Maximilian loved seafaring and distant horizons) commemorates the "brave, noble, and handsome Maximilian" as the blameless sacrificial victim demanded by the gods of the New World to avenge the crimes committed by Charles V's conquistadors, and draws a parallel between the fates of mad Joanna and the mad Charlotte. In the vault of the Capuchins in Vienna, Maximilian's body, brought back by Admiral Wilhelm von Tegetthoff, the hero of the naval Battle of Lissa, lies in a sarcophagus decorated with the Mexican coat of arms. Maximilian's wish, expressed in a beautiful poem, "I should like to die on a mountain," was not fulfilled.

Twenty years later the tragedy of the Emperor's brother and sister-in-law was followed by the suicide of his only son Rudolf at Mayerling (January 30, 1889). Almost ten years later his wife, Empress Elizabeth, was murdered by an Italian anarchist (September 10, 1898), and finally the heir, Arch-duke Francis Ferdinand, and his wife died under the bullets of Serbian conspirators at Sarajevo on June 28, 1914, and the First World War broke out. During the world conflagration that annihilated his kingdom, the aged Emperor, who had ascended the throne amid the storms of revolution, died on November 21, 1916.

In the face of the chain of catastrophes Francis Joseph seemed ever colder and more unmoved. When Francis Ferdinand's Chief of Staff told him the news of the assassination at Sarajevo and of his nephew's last moments, the Emperor immediately enquired after the progress of the recently completed maneuvers. This may appear heartless and unfeeling, but the Chief of Staff correctly interpreted it as the behavior of a man too proud to show his pain, who had learned through much misfortune to see in the preservation of his dignity and self-control, as well as in the thought of doing his duty, the one possibility of mastering a terrible destiny.

The feeling for dignity and duty finally took complete control of Francis Joseph, which accounts for his having become such a symbol of the Empire that his subordinates, and particularly his soldiers, could not conceive of Austria without him. The dynastic consciousness of the old-Habsburgs and their conviction that they were divinely predestined to govern, finally was joined harmoniously to Joseph's concept of self-sacrificing devotion to the state. Similarly, Francis Joseph's attitude to religion, the Church, and its functionaries, combined the devotion of a faithful Catholic with the consciousness of his own imperial majesty and his sovereign rights; it appeared in his treatment of dueling, and in the last veto cast by a sovereign in a papal election. Duty and honor, chivalry and uprightness, were his chief values; his embodiment of them inspired and instructed his subjects, especially in the bureaucracy and the Army. The ruler who united the names of his two predecessors, Francis and Joseph, tried to live up to the ideal of being the first Civil Servant of the State as well as a good father of his family, and in large measure he achieved it.

His successor and great-nephew Charles, who acceded at

the age of twenty-nine, was confronted by a task that could hardly have been accomplished by a stronger personality with better preparation for the role of monarch. What he did and what he left undone at the beginning of his reign testified that he was true to his convictions, honest and straightforward (he had the best intentions and, above all, a deep and sincere desire for peace), but also revealed all too clearly his lack of political and psychological experience. For this reason, he probably hastened rather than postponed the inevitable end, and both his efforts to make a separate peace and his attempt to reconstruct the monarchy at the last minute were doomed to failure. Nothing was left to him in the last hours of the old Empire but to follow the advice of his statesmen and withdraw from the exercise of government, which was, not formally but in effect, the equivalent of an abdication. In the Baroque hunting castle of Eckartsau, on the edge of the Marchfeld and not far from the place where his ancestor Rudolf won the lordship of Austria in his battle against Ottokar of Bohemia, he spent his last months (the winter of 1918–19) in his native land before a British escort took him into exile in Switzerland. Badly advised, and misunderstanding the power politics of the postwar years, he tried twice, in the spring and the autumn of 1921, to take over Hungary, which had again been declared a monarchy after the suppression of the Communist revolution. After his second attempt he was taken to the island of Madeira, where he died the following spring, on April 1, 1922.

High above the town and harbor of Funchal, in the middle of splendid southern vegetation, lies the little pilgrimage church of Our Lady of the Mountain. From here one has a sweeping view of the Atlantic, both of whose shores were governed by the Habsburgs at the zenith of their power. In a side chapel of the church stands a plain metal coffin. Its only adornment is a crown of thorns and the inscription, *Fiat Voluntas Tua*. There, under the symbol of the crown of thorns, lies the last ruler of the House of Habsburg.

15: The Habsburgs and Europe

The House of Habsburg remained a true representative of its place of origin, the heart of Europe. There is a striking parallel between the dynasty's growth in power and the importance of the continent in the world. The three centuries from 1600 to 1900 marked the zenith of European as well as Habsburg power; the House's strength began to decay when the center of power shifted from the Continent itself to the peripheral nations—England, Russia, and America. The First World War, which established Europe's decline in power, brought the end of Habsburg rule.

In the course of the centuries it had embraced many widely separated countries, from Portugal to Transylvania, from the Netherlands to Sicily. By incorporating them into a larger community, Habsburg rule helped many of the countries and peoples to flourish, although sometimes it harnessed their forces for overambitious purposes that taxed them up to and beyond their limits. The dynasty (whose members, during the centuries, corresponded with each other in Latin, German, French, Spanish, Italian, and Hungarian), combined in its own family tradition the political ideas and intellectual trends of many European peoples: the medieval concept of Empire and German national humanism, Burgundian chivalry and the Spanish ideals of racial and religious purity, the political and religious concepts of the Counter Reformation and the Baroque, the philosophies of the Italian Enlightenment and the French physiocrats, German classicism and romanticism, and finally even the ethnic nationalism of eastern Europe which, in its Hungarian, Polish, and Ukrainian forms, attracted individual members of the House. But never, not even in the time of Charles V, did the Hapsburg Empire subjugate Europe as completely as did Napoleon's French Empire or Hitler's National Socialist *Reich*—though these existed only for a comparatively brief moment in history. This fact may provide new proof of the European nature of the dynasty.

The hackneyed idea of the Habsburgs as stubborn guardians of the established order, as "lead weights in European history"—whether positive or negative—does not do justice to the widespread Habsburg efforts on behalf of reform throughout the centuries, nor to their function as intermediaries in communicating new and advanced political ideas and institutions from west to east, south to north, and back again. The view of the Habsburgs as simply the typical last survivors of the old European intellectual, social, and economic order of aristocracy and peasantry is contradicted by the fact that the members of the House of Habsburg-Lorraine consciously promoted and supported the Industrial Revolution in Central Europe, and, in so doing, remained completely within the tradition of older Habsburg economic policy. Whoever wishes to see the Habsburgs only in the glory surrounding the imperial idea of Charles V, or in their Baroque apotheosis, easily loses sight of the family's striking and characteristic political realism (from Rudolf the Ancestor down to Emperor Francis Joseph), or the sober reluctance to indulge in political adventures and the bureaucratic zeal for duty that distinguished so many members of the House. Often it seems as if the Habsburgs possessed a uniquely strong feeling for rhythm and balance, so that during revolutionary storms they inclined to conservatism, and in stagnant periods to reform and revival.

Habsburg history is in both the particular and the general sense not national but European history. From its earliest origins the family was entrusted with the task of resolving the tensions between west and east, north and south. In their success and failure, achievement and frustration, the Habsburgs laid up an enormous store of European experience—a parallel to the collections of treasures created by artists of all the European nations and put together by the connoisseurs of the family during the course of centuries. The probable value of a modern study of the European dynasty of the Habsburgs lies in putting this experience to creative use for the present and future of Europe.

Bibliography

Since Johann, Kertész, *Bibliographie der Habsburg-Literatur*, Budapest, 1934, and Mathilde Uhlirz, *Handbuch des Geschichte Oesterreichs*, 4 vols., 1927–44, list all works that appeared before their publication dates, in general only more recent literature has been included here.

1: THE HABSBURGS AND HISTORY

General surveys of Austrian—and thus also largely Habsburg—history: Hugo Hantsch, *Die Geschichte Oesterreichs*, 2 vols., 2d and 3d ed., 1951 and 1953; Heinrich Benedikt, *Monarchie der Gegensätze*, 1947. A more popular summary of Austrian history: Rudolf Kremser, *Thron zwischen Ost and West, Tausend Jahre Oesterreich*, 1956. Discussions of the basic problems of Habsburg history: Otto Brunner, "Zur Frage der österreichischen Geschichte," Mitt. d. Inst. f. Geschichtsforschung, 55, 1945; Otto Brunner, *Das Haus Oesterreich und die Donaumonarchie*, Festgabe für Harold Steinacker, Südost-Forschungen XIV, 1955. On Habsburg historiography: Anna Coreth, *Oesterreichische Geschichtsschreibung in der Barockzeit*, 1950; Alphons Lhotsky, *Geschichte des Instituts für österreichische Geschichtsforschung*, 1954; *Spectrum Austriae*, ed. by Otto Schulmeister, 1957. The elegant and beautifully designed book by Michel Dugast Rouillé, Hubert Cuny, and Baron Hervé Pinoteau, *Les grands mariages des Habsbourg*, Paris, 1955, is valuable especially because of its extensive genealogical and heraldic material, but unfortunately it also contains numerous errors and superficialities. The article by Emil Franzel, "Die Habsburger," in *Neues Abendland*, 5, 1951, attempts a summary appreciation of the dynasty.
The expert opinion of Ferdinand II's counselors is discussed in: Adam Wandruszka, *Reichspatriotismus und Reichspolitik zur Zeit des Prager Friedens von 1635*, 1955, pp. 47 ff. Pergen's memorandum is quoted by Hans Voltelini in *Gesamtdeutsche Vergangenheit*, Srbik-Festschrift, 1938. The remark by Emperor Charles is quoted by E. K. Winter, "Am Beispiel Oesterreichs," *Hochland*, 6, 1955.

2: ROMANS, TROJANS, OR ALAMANNI?

Alphons Lhotsky, "Apis Colonna, Fabeln und Theorien über die Abkunft der Habsburger," *Mitt. d. Inst. f. Geschichtsf.*, 55, 1945;

Anna Coreth, "Dynastisch-politische Ideen Kaiser Maximilians I.," *Mitt. d. öst. Staatsarchivs*, 3, 1950.

3: AT THE CROSSROADS OF THE WEST

Bruno Meyer, "Studien zum habsburgischen Hausrecht," I–IV, *Zeitschrift f. Schweizerische Geschichte*, 1945 and 1947.

4: KING RUDOLF I, THE ANCESTOR

Oswald Redlich's works, his monumental biography, *Rudolf von Habsburg*, 1903, and particularly for the subject of this chapter, his "Rudolf von Habsburg in der volkstümlichen Ueberlieferung," *Jb. f. Landeskunde v. Niederöst.*, 17/18, 1918–19, are still valid today. The most recent general discussion of Rudolf I is by Friedrich Schönstedt, in *Die grossen Deutschen*, edited by Hermann Hempel, vol. 1, 1956, pp. 217 ff.
For this and the following chapters, see especially: Theodor Mayer, "Die Habsburger am Oberrhein im Mittelalter," *Gesamtdeutsche Vergangenheit*, op. cit., and Hans Erich Feine, "Die Territorialbildung der Habsburger im deutschen Südwesten," *Ztschr. d. Sav. St. f. Rechtsgesch.*, 67, 1950, Germ. Abt.

5: FAILURE AND RENUNCIATION

On the Windisch murder: Bruno Meyer, op. cit., vol. I, 1945; on its effects in the rest of the world: Hans Hirsch, "Deutsches Königtum und römisches Kaisertum," in *Oesterreich, Erbe und Sendung*, ed. by Nadler and Srbik, 1936.
On the origins of the Swiss Confederacy: Harold Steinacker, "Staatswerdung und politische Willensbildung im Alpenraum," *Schlernschriften* 52, 1946; Bruno Meyer, "Die Entstehung der Eidgenossenschaft, Der Stand der heutigen Anschauungen," *Schweizerische Zeitschrift f. Geschichte*, 2, 1952; Harold Steinacker, "Die Habsburger und der Ursprung der Eidgenossenschaft," *MIÖG*, 61, 1953. It is worth noting that in the two last-mentioned articles both the Swiss and the Austrian historians agree that the outbreak of the conflict between the Confederacy and the Habsburgs was caused by the clash of two offensives and two expansionist drives.

6: THE "ARCH-HOUSE" AND ITS MYTHOLOGY

Otto Brunner, "Oesterreich, das Reich und der Osten im späteren Mittelalter," *Oesterreich, Erbe und Sendung*, op. cit.; Alphons

Lhotsky, "Was heisst Haus Oesterreich?" *Anzeiger d. Oest. Akad. d. Wiss.*, 1956; Ernst Karl Winter, *Rudolph IV. von Oesterreich*, 2 vols., 1934-36. See also the basic work on late medieval constitutional history, particularly in Austria, by Otto Brunner, *Land und Herrschaft*, 2d ed., 1942; Alphons Lhotsky, *Priv᾿agium Maius*, 1957.

7: DYNASTY DIVIDED

Otto Brunner, "Oesterreich . . ." op. cit.; Hans Kramer, "Die Grundlinien der Aussenpolitik Herzog Friedrich IV.," *Tiroler Heimat*, vol. 17; Hans Kramer, "Die Grundlinien der Aussenpolitik Herzog Sigmunds von Tirol," *Tiroler Heimat*, vols. 11 and 12; Alphons Lhotsky, "Die Bibliothek Kaiser Friedrichs, III.," *MIÖG*, 58, 1950; Alphons Lhotsky, "A.E.I.O.U., Die 'Devise' Kaiser Friedrichs III. und sein Notizbuch," *MIÖG*, 60, 1952.

8: THE "HOUSE OF AUSTRIA AND BURGUNDY"

Anna Coreth, "Ein Wappenbuch Kaiser Maximilians I.," *Festschrift des Haus-, Hof- und Staatsarchiv*, 1949, vol. I, pp. 219 ff.; Hellmuth Rössler, *Grösse und Tragik des christlichen Europa*, 1955, pp. 22 ff. Two recent books on Maximilian are to be considered more as historical novels: Will Winker, *Kaiser Maximilian, Zwischen Wirklichkeit und Traum*, 1950, and Ann Tizia Leitich, *Der Kaiser mit dem Granatapfel*, 1955.
For this and the following chapter, see also: Alphons Dopsch, "Die Weststaatspolitik der Habsburger im Werden ihres Grossreiches (1477 bis 1526)," *Gesamtdeutsche Vergangenheit*, op. cit.; Henri d'Hulst, *Le mariage de Philippe le Beau avec Jeanne de Castille*, Anvers, 1958.

9: HABSBURG WORLD POWER

Karl Brandi, *Kaiser Karl V.*, 2 vols., 2d ed., 1941; Peter Rassow, *Die politische Welt Karls V.*, 1942; Peter Rassow, *Forschungen zur Reichs-Idee im 16. und 17. Jahrhundert*, 1955. Especially on Charles's plans for the succession, see: Carl J. Burckhardt, *Gedanken über Karl V.*; Royall Tyler, *The Emperor Charles the Fifth*, London, 1956; Ghislaine de Boom, *Les voyages de Charles Quint*, Bruxelles, 1957.

10: MADRID AND VIENNA

On Philip II: Ludwig Pfandl, *Philipp II., Gemälde eines Lebens und einer Zeit*, 1938. On the Spanish idea of racial purity ("limpieza de sangre"): Américo Castro, *La realidad histórica de España*, Mexico,

1954, pp. 496 ff., "Limpieza de sangre e Inquisicion." For the report of Ambassador Corraro on the sons of Maximilian II: "Relationen venetianischer Botschafter über Deutschland und Oesterreich im 16. Jahrhundert," ed. by J. Fiedler, *Fontes rerum austriacarum* XXX, 1870, p. 336. Hans Sturmberger, *Georg Erasmus Tschernembl*, 1953; Grete Mecenseffy, *Habsburger im 17. Jahrhundert. Die Beziehungen der Höfe von Wien und Madrid während des Dreissigjährigen Krieges, Archiv f. öst. Geschichte,* 121, 1955; Grete Mecenseffy, *Geschichte des Protestantismus in Oesterreich,* 1956; Alphons Lhotsky, *Die Geschichte der Sammlungen,* Festschrift des Kunsthistorischen Museums, 1945.

11: THE RULERS DURING THE AUSTRIAN BAROQUE PERIOD

Anna Coreth, *Pietas Austriaca, Wesen und Bedeutung habsburgischer Frömmigkeit in der Barockzeit, Mitt. d. öst. Staatsarchivs* 7, 1954; Taras von Borodajkewycz, "Die Kirche in Oesterreich," in *Oesterreich, Erbe und Sendung,* op. cit.; Heinrich Ritter von Srbik, *Wallensteins Ende,* 2d ed., 1952; Wandruszka, *Reichspatriotismus,* op. cit. For the political influence of the Jesuit Lamormain, confessor to Ferdinand II, see Andreas Posch, "Zur Tätigkeit und Beurteilung Lamormains," *MIÖG* 63, 1955. A basic work on the education of princes in the Baroque period is the summary "Mirror for princes," "Princeps in compendio," sometimes ascribed to Emperor Ferdinand II, and edited by Oswald Redlich in *Monatsbl. f. Lkde. v. Niederösterr.* 3, 1906–7. Hans Sturmberger, *Kaiser Ferdinand II. und das Problem des Absolutismus,* 1957. Hans Kramer, "Herzog Karl V. von Lothringen und Königinwitwe Eleonore in Tirol," *MIÖG* 62, 1954. On Joseph I: Wilhelm Bauer's posthumously published study, *Joseph I, Mitt. d. Oberöst. Landesarchivs* 4, 1955. On Charles VI: Oswald Redlich, "Die Tagebücher Karls VI.," *Gesamtdeutsche Vergangenheit,* op. cit.; Oswald Redlich, *Das Werden einer Grossmacht,* 1938. On Charles VI's dream of the Spanish kingdom and the activity and significance of the "Consejo de España" in Vienna, see Peter Gasser, *Das spanische Königtum Karls VI. in Wien, Mitt. d. öst. Staatsarchivs* 6, 1953.

12: THE GREAT EMPRESS

Friedrich Walter, *Männer um Maria Theresia,* 1951; Heinrich Kretschmayr, *Maria Theresia,* 1938; Alexander Novotny, *Staatskanzler Kaunitz als geistige Persönlichkeit,* 1947; Edith Kotasek, *Feldmarschall Graf Lacy, Ein Leben für Oesterreichs Heer,* 1956; *Maria Theresias politisches Testament,* ed. by Josef Kallbrunner, 1952; Richard Raithel, *Maria Theresia und Joseph II. ohne Purpur. Mit ihren eigenen*

Worten und denen ihrer Zeitgenossen geschildert, 1954; Erika Weinzierl-Fischer, *Die Bekämpfung der Hungersnot in Böhem 1770–72 durch Maria Theresia und Joseph II.*, *Mitt. d. öst. Staatsarchivs* 7, 1954; *Maria Theresia in ihren Briefen und Staatsschriften*, ed. by Ludwig Jedlicka, 1955; Peter Reinhold, *Maria Theresia*, 1957; Adam Wandruszka, *Le istruzioni di Francesco di Lorena per il figlio Leopoldo*, *Archivio storico Italiano*, 1957.

13: SERVANTS OF THE STATE

On Joseph II: Eduard Winter, *Josef II. Von den geistigen Quellen und letzten Beweggründen seiner Reformideen*, 1946; Nicholas Henderson, "Joseph II," *History Today*, 5, 1955, pp. 613–21.
On *Josephinismus*: Eduard Winter, *Der Josefinismus und seine Geschichte*, 1943; Fritz Valjavec, *Der Josephinismus*, 1944; Ferdinand Maass, *Der Josephinismus*, *Quellen zu seiner Geschichte in Oesterreich*, 4 vols. published, 1951–57. A detailed bibliography is provided by Fridolin Dörrer, "Römische Stimmen zum Frühjosephinismus," *MIÖG* 63, 1955.
On Leopold II: Heinz Holldack, "Die Neutralitätspolitik Leopolds von Toskana," *Hist. Vjschr.*, 30, 1936; Heinz Holldack, "Die Reformpolitik Leopolds von Toskana," *HZ*. 165, 1942. Leopold's "confession of faith" is quoted from Alphons Huber, *Die Politik Kaiser Josephs II., beurteilt von seinem Bruder Leopold von Toskana*, 1877. Archduke Albert's memorandum to Crenneville is from Heinrich Ritter von Srbik, "Erzherzog Albrecht, Benedek und der altösterreichische Soldatengeist," *Aus Oesterreichs Vergangenheit*, 1949.
Reinhold Lorenz, *Erzherzog Carl als Denker*, 1941; Viktor Bibl, *Erzherzog Karl*, 1942; Viktor Theiss, *Erzherzog Johann, der steirische Prinz*, 1950; Jean de Bourgoing, *Marie Louise von Oesterreich*, 1949. Walter Consuelo Langsam, *Francis the Good*, 1949.

14: THE CROWN OF THORNS

The trilogy on Francis Joseph by Egon Caesar Conte Corti, *Vom Kind zum Kaiser*, 1951; *Mensch und Herrscher*, 1952; *Der alte Kaiser*, 1955 (completed after Corti's death by Hans Sokol). *Briefe Kaiser Franz Josephs an Frau Katharina Schratt*, ed. by Jean de Bourgoing, 1949. The best short appreciation of Francis Joseph's personality remains Heinrich Ritter von Srbik's article, "Franz Joseph I., Charakter und Regierungsgrundsätze," *Aus Oesterreichs Vergangenheit*, 1949. On the tragedy of Maximilian of Mexico: Richard Blaas, "Die Gedächtniskapelle in Querétaro," *Mitt. d. öst. Staatsarchivs*, 8, 1955. On Francis Ferdinand: Rudolf Kiszling, *Erzherzog Franz Ferdinand*

von Oesterreich-Este, 1953; supplementary material is contained in: Friedrich Funder, *Vom Gestern ins Heute*, 1952; Johann Christoph Allmayer-Beck, *Ministerpräsident Baron Beck*, 1956.
On Archduke Eugene: Adolf L. Vischer, "Erzherzog Eugen," *Basler Jahrbuch*, 1956, pp. 130 ff.; Hans Kramer, "Feldmarschall Erzherzog Eugen und Alttirol," *Der Schlern*, 1957.
Géza Kövess, "Die Nachkommen des Kaisers Franz Joseph I.," *Adler*, August 1948.
The quotations from Francis Joseph are taken from Srbik, op. cit.; Paul Müller, "Auswärtige Politik Oesterreichs," *Oesterreich, Erbe und Sendung*, op. cit.; Otto Brunner, *Das Haus Habsburg und die Donaumonarchie*, op. cit. (quoted from C. J. Burckhardt).

Books in English

(Bibliography especially prepared for the
American edition)

GENERAL

Coxe, W. *History of the House of Austria, 1215–1848*. 4th ed. London: George Bell & Sons, Ltd., 1882. 4 vols.

Frischauer, Paul. *The Imperial Crown: The Story of the Rise and Fall of the Holy Roman and the Austrian Empires*. Tr. by H. Leigh Farnell. London: Cassell & Co., Ltd., 1939.

Kann, Robert A. *The Habsburg Empire: A Study in Integration and Disintegration*. New York: Frederick A. Praeger, Inc., 1957.

Macartney, Carlile Aylmer. *Hungary*. London: Ernest Benn, Ltd., 1934.

Seton-Watson, R. W. *A History of the Czechs and Slovaks*. London: Hutchinson & Co., Ltd., 1943.

MEDIEVAL

Leeper, A. W. A. *A History of Medieval Austria*. Ed. by R. W. Seton-Watson and C. A. Macartney. New York: Oxford University Press, 1941.

NINETEENTH / TWENTIETH CENTURIES

Colquhoun, Archibald Ross. *The Whirlpool of Europe: Austria-Hungary and the Habsburgs*. London: Harper & Brothers, 1907.

Gooch, George Peabody. *Before the War: Studies in Diplomacy*. New York: Longmans, Green & Co., Inc., 1936–38. 2 vols.

Jászi, Oscar. *The Dissolution of the Habsburg Monarchy*. Chicago: The University of Chicago Press, 1929; Phoenix paperback, 1961.

Jelavich, Charles and Barbara. *The Habsburg Monarchy: Toward a Multinational Empire or National States?* New York: Holt, Rhinehart & Winston Co., Inc., 1959.

Kann, Robert A. *The Multinational Empire: Nationalism and National Reform in the Habsburg Monarchy, 1848–1918*. New York: Columbia University Press, 1950. 2 vols.

Kohn, Hans. *The Habsburg Empire, 1804–1918*. Princeton: D. Van Nostrand Co., Inc., 1961. Anvil paperback.

Langer, William L. *The Diplomacy of Imperialism, 1890–1902*. New York: Alfred A. Knopf, Inc., 1935. 2 vols.

———. *European Alliances and Alignments, 1871–1890*. New York: Alfred A. Knopf, Inc., 1931.

Leger, L. P. M., and W. E. Lingelbach. *Austria-Hungary*. New York, 1913.

Macartney, Carlile Aylmer. *Problems of the Danube Basin*. London: Cambridge University Press, 1942.

May, Arthur J. *The Hapsburg Monarchy, 1867–1914*. Cambridge: Harvard University Press, 1951.

Pribram, Alfred F. *Austria-Hungary and Great Britain, 1908–1914*, Tr. by Ian F. D. Morrow. London: Oxford University Press, 1951.

———. *Austrian Foreign Policy, 1908–1918*. London, 1923.

———. *The Secret Treaties of Austria-Hungary, 1879–1914*. Cambridge: Harvard University Press, 1920–22. 2 vols.

Rath, Reuben John. *The Viennese Revolution of 1848*. Austin: The University of Texas Press, 1957.

Steed, Henry Wickham. *The Doom of the Hapsburgs*. Bristol, England: J. W. Arrowsmith, Ltd., 1937.

———. *The Hapsburg Monarchy*. 4th ed. London: Constable & Co., Ltd., 1919.

Taylor, Alan John Percivale. *The Habsburg Monarchy, 1809–1918: A History of the Austrian Empire and Austria-Hungary*. New ed. London: Hamish Hamilton, Ltd., 1948.

Zeman, Zbynek A. B. *The Break-up of the Habsburg Empire, 1914–1918: A Study in National and Social Revolution*. London, New York: Oxford University Press, 1961.

MAXIMILIAN I

Seton-Watson, R. W. *Maximilian I, Holy Roman Emperor*. London: Constable & Co., Ltd., 1902.

CHARLES V

Armstrong, Edward. *The Emperor Charles V*. London: Macmillan and Co., Ltd., 1910. 2 vols.

Brandi, Karl. *The Emperor Charles V: The Growth and Destiny of a Man and of a World Empire*. Tr. by C. V. Wedgwood. London: Jonathan Cape, Ltd., 1939.

Lewis, D. B. Wyndham. *Charles of Europe*. New York: Coward-McCann, Inc., 1931.

McElwee, William Lloyd. *The Reign of Charles V, 1516–1558*. London: Macmillan & Co., Ltd., 1936.

Tyler, Royall. *The Emperor Charles the Fifth*. Fair Lawn, New Jersey: Essential Books, Inc., 1956.

PHILIP II

Cadoux, Cecil John. *Philip of Spain and the Netherlands: An Essay on Moral Judgments in History*. London: Lutherworth Press, 1947.

Hume, Martin Andrew Sharp. *Philip II of Spain*. London: Macmillan and Co., Ltd., 1906.

Loth, David Goldsmith. *Philip II of Spain*. New York: Brentano's, 1932.

Prescott, William Hickling. *History of the Reign of Philip the Second, King of Spain.* Boston: Phillips, Sampson, 1855–58. 3 vols.

Simpson, Helen de Guerry. *The Spanish Marriage.* London: Peter Davies, Ltd., 1933.

Walsh, William Thomas. *Philip II.* London and New York: Sheed & Ward, Inc., 1937.

MARIA THERESA

Bright, James Franck. *Life of Maria Theresa.* New York: The Macmillan Company, 1897.

Goldsmith, Margaret Leland. *Maria Theresa of Austria.* London: Arthur Barker, Ltd., 1936.

Gooch, George Peabody. *Maria Theresa and Other Studies.* London: Longmans, Green & Co., Inc., 1951.

Mahan, J. Alexander. *Maria Theresa of Austria.* New York: The Thomas Y. Crowell Co., 1932.

Morris, Constance Lily. *Maria Theresa, the Last Conservative.* New York: Alfred A. Knopf, Inc., 1937.

JOSEPH II

Gooch, George Peabody. *Maria Theresa and Other Studies.* London: Longmans, Green & Co., Inc., 1951.

Padover, S. K. *The Revolutionary Emperor, Joseph the Second.* New York: David Kemp & Co., 1934.

Wangermann, Ernst. *From Joseph II to the Jacobin Trials: Government Policy and Public Opinion in the Habsburg Dominions in the Period of the French Revolution.* London: Oxford University Press, 1959.

FRANCIS I

Langsam, Walter C. *Francis the Good. Vol. 1: The Education of an Emperor, 1768–1792.* New York: The Macmillan Company, 1949.

FRANCIS JOSEPH

Bagger, Eugene Szekeres. *Francis Joseph, Emperor of Austria, King of Hungary.* New York and London: G. P. Putnam's Sons, 1927.

Clark, Chester W. *Franz Joseph and Bismarck: The Diplomacy of Austria before the War of 1866.* Cambridge: Harvard University Press, 1934.

Corti, Egon C. *Elizabeth, Empress of Austria.* Tr. by Catherine Alison Phillips. New Haven: Yale University Press, 1936.

Hallberg, Charles William. *Franz Joseph and Napoleon III, 1852–1864: A Study of Austro-French Relations.* New York: Bookman Associates, Inc., 1955.

Harding, Bertita. *Golden Fleece: The Story of Franz Joseph and Elizabeth of Austria.* Indianapolis and New York: Bobbs-Merrill Co., 1937.

Margutti, Albert. *Emperor Francis Joseph and His Times.* London: Hutchinson & Co., 1921.

Redlich, Joseph. *Emperor Francis Joseph of Austria: A Biography.* New York: The Macmillan Company, 1929.

Rupp, George H. *A Wavering Friendship: Russia and Austria, 1876–1878.* Cambridge: Harvard University Press, 1941.

Steed, Henry Wickham. *The Doom of the Hapsburgs.* Bristol, England: J. W. Arrowsmith, Ltd., 1937.

Tschuppik, Karl. *The Empress Elizabeth of Austria.* Tr. by Eric Sutton. New York: Brentano's, 1930.

———. *The Reign of the Emperor Francis Joseph, 1848–1916.* Tr. by C. J. S. Sprigge. London: George Bell & Sons, Ltd., 1930.

RUDOLF, CROWN PRINCE

Barkeley, Richard. *The Road to Mayerling: Life and Death of Crown Prince Rudolph of Austria.* London and New York: St Martin's Press, Inc., 1958.

Lonyay, Count Carl. *Rudolph, the Tragedy of Mayerling.* New York: Charles Scribner's Sons, 1949.

Mitis, Oskar von. *The Life of the Crown Prince Rudolph of Habsburg. . . .* Tr. by M. H. Jerome and Eileen O'Connor. London: Skeffington and Son, Ltd., 1930.

CHARLES I

Polzer-Hoditz, Count Arthur. *The Emperor Karl.* Tr. by D. F. Tait and F. S. Flint. Boston: Houghton Mifflin Company, 1930.

Vivian, Herbert. *The Life of the Emperor Charles of Austria.* London: Grayson & Grayson, Ltd., 1932.

Genealogical Tables

The genealogical tables are intended to provide the reader with a general survey. There has been no attempt to make them complete, which would have been impossible within this compass, especially because in almost all centuries the Habsburgs were distinguished for their fecundity. (Rudolf I had eleven children, Albert I thirteen, Ferdinand I fifteen, Maximilian II sixteen, Archduke Charles of Central Austria fifteen, Maria Theresa sixteen, Leopold II sixteen, Archduchess Marie Valerie—Emperor Francis Joseph's daughter, who married her cousin, Archduke Francis Salvator—ten, and Emperor Charles eight.) In Table III the proper genealogical order of brothers and sisters, reading from left to right according to date of birth, has not always been followed, in order to bring out the interrelationships between the Madrid and Viennese lines. Among the children of Charles of Central Austria, Margaret was younger than Ferdinand II, and among the children of Philip IV of Spain the Infanta Margaret Theresa was older than Charles II.

The names of emperors and kings have been printed in capitals.

For the numerous progeny of Emperor Francis Joseph's daughters Gisela and Marie Valerie, and his granddaughter Elizabeth, see the work by Géza Kövess cited in the bibliography to Chapter 14.

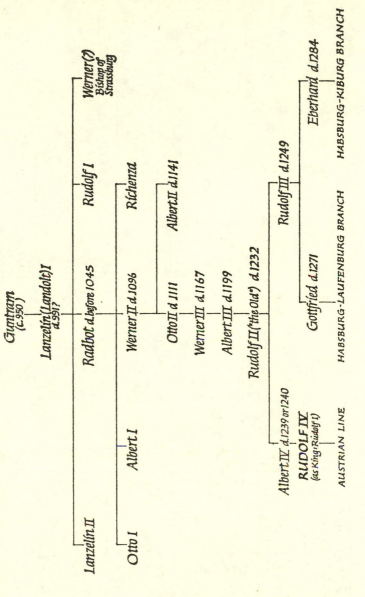

Guntram
(c.950)

Lanzelin (Landolt) I
d.991?

Lanzelin II

Otto I

Albert I

Radbot d.before 1045

Werner II d.1096

Otto II d.1111

Werner III d.1167

Albert III d.1199

Rudolf II ("the Old") d.1232

Albert IV d.1239 or 1240

RUDOLF IV
(as King Rudolf I)

AUSTRIAN LINE

Rudolf I

Richenza

Albert II d.1141

Gottfried d.1271

HABSBURG-LAUFENBURG BRANCH

Rudolf III d.1249

Eberhard d.1284

HABSBURG-KIBURG BRANCH

Werner (?)
Bishop of
Strassburg

GENEALOGICAL TABLE II
From Rudolf I to Maximilian I

RUDOLF I d.1291
1. Gertrude (Anna) von Hohenberg   2. Elizabeth (Agnes) of Burgundy

ALBERT I d.1308
Elizabeth of Tyrol

Hartmann d.1281

Rudolf III d.1290
Agnes of Bohemia

John the Patricide d.1313

FREDERICK I
('the Handsome')
d.1330
Elizabeth of Aragon

Leopold I
d.1326

Otto d.1339

Leopold II d.1344

Albert II
d.1358
Joanna von Pfirt

Frederick II d.1344

Rudolf III d.1307
1. Blanche of France
2. Elizabeth of Bohemia

ALBERTINE LINE

LEOPOLDINE LINE

TYROLEAN LINE

Frederick III
d.1362

Albert III d.1395
1. Elizabeth of Luxemburg
2. Beatrice of Hohenzollern

Leopold III
d.1386
Virida Visconti

Frederick IV d.1439
1. Elizabeth of
the Palatinate
2. Anne of Brunswick

Sigmund d.1496
Abdicated 1490
1. Eleanor of Scotland
2. Catherine of Saxony

Rudolf IV d.1365·
Catherine of Luxemburg

William
d.1406
Joanna of
Naples-Anjou

Leopold IV
d.1411
Catherine
of Burgundy

Ernest the Iron
Duke d.1424
1. Margaret of
Pomerania
2. Cymburgis of
Masovia

Albert IV d.1404
Joanna of Bavaria

ALBERT V (II) d.1439
Elizabeth of Luxemburg

FREDERICK V (III)
d.1493
Leonora (Helena)
of Portugal

Albert VI
d.1463

Ladislas Posthumus
d.1457

MAXIMILIAN I
d.1519

GENEALOGICAL TABLE III
From Maximilian I to Maria Theresa

MAXIMILIAN I d.1519
1. Mary of Burgundy (Daughter of Charles the Bold)
2. Bianca Maria Sforza

PHILIP I d.1506 — Joanna of Spain

SPANISH LINE | AUSTRIAN LINE

FERDINAND I d.1564 — Anne of Bohemia and Hungary

CHARLES V d.1558 — Isabella of Portugal

Charles of Central Austria d.1590 — Mary Anne of Bavaria

MAXIMILIAN II d.1576

Ferdinand of Tyrol d.1595 — Philippine Welser

Maria

PHILIP II d.1598
1. Mary of Portugal (Mother of Don Carlos)
2. Mary Tudor
3. Isabella of Valois
4. Anne, daughter of Maximilian II

RUDOLF II d.1612

MATTHIAS d.1619

Maximilian d.1618

Albert d.1621

YOUNGER TYROLEAN LINE
Leopold d.1632 — Claudia de Medici

FERDINAND II d.1637
1. Mary Anne of Bavaria
2. Eleanor of Gonzaga

PHILIP III d.1621 — Margaret, daughter of Charles of Central Austria

Ferdinand Charles d.1662 — Anna de Medici

Sigmund Francis d.1665

FERDINAND III d.1657 — Mary Anne

PHILIP IV d.1665
1. Isabella of France
2. Mary Anne, daughter of Ferdinand III

LEOPOLD I d.1705
1. Margaret Theresa
2. Claudia Felicitas
3. Eleanor of Pfalz-Neuburg

CHARLES II d.1700

JOSEPH I d.1711 — Amalia Wilhelmine of Brunswick-Lüneburg

CHARLES VI d.1740 — Elizabeth Christine of Brunswick-Lüneburg-Wolfenbüttel

MARIA THERESA d.1780

GENEALOGICAL TABLE IV
The House of Habsburg-Lorraine

MARIA THERESA 1736 **FRANCIS STEPHEN** of Lorraine
(Emperor Francis I) d.1765
d.1780

JOSEPH II
d.1790
1 Isabella of
Bourbon-Parma
2 Mary Josepha
of Bavaria

Mary Christine
d.1798
Albert of
Saxony-Teschen

LEOPOLD II
d.1792
Mary Louise of
Bourbon-Spain

Mary Caroline
d.1814
Ferdinand of
Bourbon-Naples

Ferdinand
d.1806
Mary Beatrix
of Modena-Este

Marie Antoinette
d.1793
Louis XVI of France

Maximilian Francis
Prince Elector of
Cologne d.1801

Maria Ludovica
(m. Francis II)

FRANCIS II (I)
d.1835
1 Elizabeth of
Württemberg
2. Maria Theresa of
Bourbon-Naples*
3 Maria Ludovica
of Modena
4. Caroline Augusta
of Bavaria

Ferdinand III
of Tuscany d.1824
1 Louise of
Bourbon-Naples
2 Mary of Saxony

Charles
d.1847
Henrietta of
Nassau-Weilburg

Maria Theresa
(m. Francis II)

Joseph
d.1847
1. Alexandra of
Russia.
2 Hermine of
Anhalt
3. Maria Dorothea
of Württemberg

John
d.1859
Anna Plochl
(Countess of
Meran)

Rainer
d.1853
Mary Elizabeth
of Savoy

Ludwig
d.1864

HABSBURG-TUSCAN LINE

LINE OF ARCHDUKE JOSEPH

LINE OF ARCHDUKE RAINER

FERDINAND I
d.1875
abdicated 1848

Francis Charles
d.1878
Sophie of Bavaria

Albert
d.1895
Hildegard of Bavaria

Charles Ferdinand
d.1874
Elizabeth, daughter

Mary Louise d.1847
Duchess of Parma
Napoleon I

FRANCIS JOSEPH I
d.1916
Elizabeth of Bavaria

Ferdinand Maximilian
Emperor of Mexico
d.1867
Charlotte of Belgium

Charles Ludwig
d.1896
1. Margaret of Saxony
2. Maria Annunciata
of Bourbon-Naples *
3. Maria Theresa of
Portugal

Ludwig Victor
d.1919

Frederick
d.1936
Isabella,
Princess Croy

Eugene
d.1954

Rudolf d.1889
Stephanie of
Belgium

Elizabeth d.1963
1. Otto, Prince of
Windischgrätz
2. Leopold Petznek

Francis Ferdinand
d.1914
Sophie, Countess
Chotek, Duchess of
Hohenberg

(Dukes of Hohenberg)

Otto Francis Joseph
d.1906
Mary Josepha of Saxony

CHARLES I d.1922
Zita of Bourbon-Parma

Otto
Regina of
Saxony-Meiningen

Adelheid

Robert
Margaret of
Savoy

Felix
Anne, Duchess
of Arenberg

Charles Ludwig
Jolande de Ligne

Rudolf
Xenia, Countess
Tschernitschew

Charlotte
George, Duke
of Mecklenburg-
Strelitz

Elizabeth
Henry of
Lichtenstein

* Mother of children listed

Name Index